CANADA

TORONTO

DETROIT

BOSTON

NEW YORK

PHILADELPHIA

Atlantic
Ocean

Sargasso
Sea

BAHAMAS

NA

CUBA

DAIQUIRÍ

BRITISH VIRGIN ISLANDS

JOST VAN DYKE

JAMAICA

NGSTON

SAN JUAN

ANTIGUA AND BARBUDA

DOMINICA

Lesser Antilles

RAS

Caribbean

PUERTO
RICO

BARBADOS

CARAGUA

COLÓN Sea

BRIDGETOWN

PORT OF SPAIN

TRINIDAD AND TOBAGO

CA

PANAMA

VENEZUELA

GUYANA

COLOMBIA

SOUTH

EQUADOR

AMERICA

PERU

BRAZIL

LIMA

AROUND THE WORLD IN 80 COCKTAILS

THIS BOOK IS DEDICATED TO THE
MEMORY OF ELIZABETH CAPLICE,
WHO SHOWED ME JUST HOW MUCH
MEANING CAN BE CONTAINED IN A
SMALL GLASS OF MIXED BOOZE.

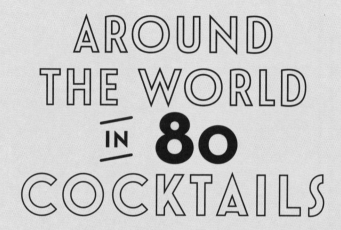

AROUND THE WORLD IN 80 COCKTAILS

CHAD PARKHILL

WITH ILLUSTRATIONS BY

ALICE OEHR

hardie grant books

CONTENTS

INTRODUCTION

Travel has always been a part of the cocktail's DNA. Early cocktail recipes called for American whiskey, British gin (itself a Dutch invention), Caribbean rum, French brandy, Italian vermouth, Spanish sherry and Portuguese madeira, among others. As travel and commerce have made the world smaller and better connected, the world of cocktails and mixed drinks has only become more diverse and – if you'll excuse the pun – more cosmopolitan. Cocktail bars around the world now sling drinks made from ingredients as diverse as Mexican tequila and mezcal, Norwegian aquavit, Peruvian or Chilean pisco, Japanese sake, Brazilian cachaça, and Chinese baijiu.

It's perhaps appropriate, then, that the very earliest origins of the cocktail show a category of drinks in transit. The earliest known use of the term 'cocktail' to refer to a drink, according to drinks historians Anistatia Miller and Jared Brown, comes from a newspaper article printed in Britain in 1798, yet only a few years later the term had leapt across the Atlantic. The cocktail itself grew up in the United States throughout the 19th century, making a few sorties out into the wider world where it was received with rapture and wonderment: at the 1867 Exposition Universelle de Paris, the American bar went through more than 500 bottles of sherry a day to keep up with Parisians' demand for Sherry Cobblers. Meanwhile, in the United States, the cocktail bartender was becoming a figure of legend – the most famous of whom, Jerry Thomas, earned more each year while at the peak of his powers than Vice President Hannibal Hamlin.

The event that truly pushed the cocktail out into the wider world, however, was Prohibition – the 'noble experiment' that effectively banned the consumption of alcohol in the United States from 1920 to 1933. Well-heeled Americans with the means to quench their thirsts in Paris, London or Havana brought the demand for cocktails with them, and bartenders faced with sudden unemployment in the United States soon found that their career could be lucrative elsewhere. While the cocktail died an undignified death in the United States, reduced to a means of masking the unpleasant taste of bathtub gin and other illicit hooch, it simultaneously blossomed elsewhere. By the time Prohibition was repealed in 1933, the cocktail had become, for better or worse, a global phenomenon.

The global expansion of the cocktail had its benefits: new ingredients, flavours and sensibilities all found their way into the glass. Not every change was beneficial, of course: during the 1970s and 1980s, the cocktail took a few unfortunate new forms, as anyone who has ever sipped a Sex on the Beach can attest. Yet while the cocktail entered a fallow period in the United States and elsewhere in the second half of the 20th century, a number of bartenders around the world were rediscovering pre-Prohibition recipes and techniques. (These had never left Japanese bartending, which later functioned as something of a time capsule.) When these recipes and techniques were introduced to a United States bar scene primed for a break from syrupy-sweet vodka-based concoctions, the global craft cocktail renaissance began in earnest. Thanks to the internet, bartenders around the world could easily share knowledge and inspiration – and now it is perfectly possible to find an expertly crafted cocktail nearly anywhere you'd care to look.

This book traces the cocktail's journey around the world, from the early 19th century through to the 21st. Each of the 80 cocktails collected here is linked to a place – sometimes literally, and sometimes more metaphorically. The Mai Tai, for instance, wasn't invented in Tahiti – but it has a lot more to do with Tahiti, or at least the *idea* of Tahiti, than it does with its actual birthplace. And each of these places, in turn, has influenced the history of drinking. I hope to show in these 80 thumbnail sketches how the cocktail changed and evolved as it racked up frequent flyer miles: what local influences it picked up and what local traditions it tapped into. Most of all, I hope to tell the colourful stories behind how some of our most beloved mixed drinks – and the new classics making their debut in these pages – came to be.

HOW TO USE THIS BOOK

Recipes

The recipes included in this book are not meant to be taken as the definitive versions of these drinks, nor the most historically accurate. As any working bartender knows, no recipe is set in stone, and recipes often need tweaking to account for any number of variables.

As you begin making these drinks at home you will soon discover some of the peculiarities of your own tastes, and you will start to discover creative methods of getting around the limitations of your liquor cabinet. Consider these recipes, then, as a starting point for your own experimentation. After all, one of the hallmarks of a classic cocktail is that it can withstand a fair amount of tweaking and still retain its identity. Just be mindful that if you start substituting ingredients you may end up with something so far removed from the original that it will bear no resemblance.

Ingredients

What materials you can access to make cocktails will depend on both your budget and your location. While the spirits business has always been a global one, not everything can be found everywhere – and import duties and other tax peculiarities mean that what is cheap somewhere might be prohibitively expensive elsewhere. For this reason, the recipes in this book avoid calling for specific brands of products wherever possible, although they may suggest certain brands of product when a generic descriptor such as 'dark rum' isn't specific enough to convey the kind of flavour profile required.

There's an old saw that a cocktail is only as good as its worst ingredient, which many budding mixologists take to mean that a good cocktail should only be mixed with the finest, and priciest, ingredients available. While this is true in an obvious sense – a Martini made from bottom-shelf gin and spoiled vermouth isn't much fun to drink – this advice obscures the fact that not all products are 'team players' that mix well with others. It also ignores the fact that, while very cheap ingredients are almost never good, the obverse isn't true: the shelves of your local liquor store are probably groaning under the weight of rather expensive products whose cost can be chalked up to clever marketing and fancy packaging rather than intrinsic quality.

An unpretentious London dry gin and a high-quality but relatively orthodox sweet vermouth will make a better Negroni than an expensive gin made from recherché botanicals and a pricey sweet vermouth loaded with bold, dominating flavours. For this reason, when a recipe in this book calls for a generic ingredient – like 'white rum' or 'tequila' – you should reach for a high-quality product that remains relatively faithful to the ingredient's general form. Having said that, experimenting with unusual products in classic cocktails is tremendous fun – as long as you're willing to accept that not every experiment will work!

For juices and other non-alcoholic components, remember that fresh is always best (particularly for lime and lemon juice, which degrade terribly when bottled), and that nobody likes flat sparkling water or flat ginger ale, so buy these in single-serve bottles or cans. Some specialty syrups that are common in bars – such as orgeat and grenadine – can be made at home using recipes found on the internet or, alternatively, you can purchase these online.

SIMPLE SYRUP

Some recipes in this book call for 'simple syrup', which is a simple mixture of water and sugar. While debate rages in cocktail circles about the merits of different ratios of sugar to water, when the recipes in this book call for simple syrup, they call for a syrup made from one part fine white sugar to one part water. To make this at home, simply combine equal parts (by volume, not weight) of sugar and piping hot water, and stir until the sugar is dissolved. This can be kept in a clean container in the fridge for a week or so, although it's so cheap and easy to make that you may find it easier to make small quantities as needed and discard the excess.

Equipment

It's tempting to spend a lot of money on fancy bar equipment for the home, but you can make most cocktails in this book without investing large sums in specialised gear. A well-balanced Manhattan made with high-quality ingredients will  taste just as delicious whether it's been mixed in a jug found in a thrift store or a handmade cut-crystal Yarai mixing glass, and if you have limited funds it's better to spend them on quality ingredients.

There are a few essentials you'll need before you start slinging drinks at home, though. Possibly the best investment you can make is a set of precise and reliable jiggers (pictured above). Look for narrow, tall ones, which have a lower margin of error than stout, wide ones. Your jigger or jiggers should be able to measure common increments for cocktail recipes: 7 ml (¼ fl oz), 15 ml (½ fl oz), 22 ml (¾ fl oz), 30 ml (1 fl oz), 45 ml (1½ fl oz) and 60 ml (2 fl oz). A bar spoon that holds a precise volume in its bowl – 5 ml (¼ fl oz) is the industry standard – is also useful, but can be replaced by an accurate teaspoon measure. For this book's purposes, a 'dash' is a very small quantity of liquid – about 1 ml (⅛ fl oz).

A Japanese-style bitters bottle with a dasher top is a useful tool for measuring ingredients that come in bottles without built-in dashers, such as absinthe or maraschino liqueur.

A decent cocktail shaker (pictured below) is a must, and professional bartenders tend to prefer two-piece 'tin on tin' shakers to other options because they are easy to clean, have no breakable glass parts and are less fiddly than three-piece cobbler shakers with built-in strainers. You can, of course, improvise with jam jars and so on, but results will vary drastically. You'll need a matching Hawthorne strainer (the one with the coiled spring, pictured on the opposite page) and a separate fine-mesh strainer (also known as a tea strainer) for removing little chips of ice and bits of juice pulp from the mix.

A good mixing glass and a high-quality bar spoon (pictured on the opposite page) are an absolute pleasure to use for stirred drinks, but by no means necessary – you can get very similar results from the larger half of a two-piece cocktail shaker and a plastic chopstick. Similarly, the insistence

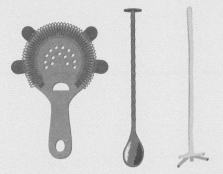

on using a julep strainer (a perforated round disc similar to a slotted spoon) for stirred drinks is something of a bartender's shibboleth: it gets you some cocktail-nerd gravitas, but it won't make your drinks any better than if you strain them with a Hawthorne strainer.

If you don't have a source of large, solid ice cubes, consider acquiring a specialised ice-cube tray for this purpose – the better the ice you use, the better your cocktails will be. Look for a tray that makes cubes of about 2.5 cm (1 in) diameter, and fill it with filtered water rather than tap for best results. For drinks that call for crushed ice, you'll need a Lewis bag (or a thick, sealable plastic bag, in a pinch) and a mallet with which to crush the ice, and in some cases a wooden swizzle stick (a branch from the *Quararibea turbinata* tree with radiating spokes at one end, pictured above) with which to swizzle the drink, or a bar spoon with a flat disc on the end. The plastic stirring rods known

STOCKING THE BAR

THE BASICS
aromatic bitters
cognac or other high-quality brandy
dry gin
dry sparkling wine
maraschino liqueur
orange bitters
orange curaçao or triple sec
rum, dark
rum, white
sweet red vermouth

SPECIALTY ITEMS
absinthe
dry vermouth
Bénédictine
bourbon whiskey
Campari
Fernet-Branca
Peychaud's bitters
sherry, light dry (manzanilla or fino)
sherry, rich dry (amontillado, palo cortado, or oloroso)
rye whiskey

BARTENDER'S TIP: Wine, sherry and vermouth will all spoil rapidly if left open at room temperature. To ensure the longevity of these ingredients, store them in your fridge.

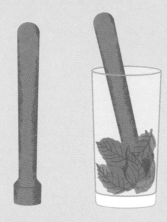

Technique

Once you've acquired the ingredients you need and have the basic equipment, you can start to put together your drinks. Although directions like 'build', 'shake' and 'stir' seem self-explanatory, a little education about proper techniques will make your life much easier and make the resulting drinks much better.

Measuring and building

To measure the components of your cocktail, start by holding the appropriate jigger on an even level in your non-dominant hand. Pour your booze, syrup or juice right up to the top of the jigger (or, if your jigger has this feature, right up to the internal measuring line for the quantity desired). Then, in one swift and fluid motion, tip the contents of your jigger into your shaker, mixing glass, or glass. Next, measure out and add the next ingredient – this is called 'building' the drink. You may find it easier to add ingredients from smallest to largest quantities – that way, if you make a mistake, you won't sacrifice too much booze. Whether you're shaking, stirring or simply building your drink in the glass, you'll get better results if you add ice at the last possible moment – this prevents the different ingredients from diluting at different rates.

as 'swizzle sticks' are pretty in highballs and tiki drinks, but they're not very useful for actual swizzling.

If you don't already have a citrus juicer, you'll need one to get the juice out of limes, lemons, oranges and grapefruits. Most bartenders swear by the 'Mexican elbow' style of hand citrus press, although these are not particularly well suited to larger fruits such as grapefruits and oranges. For these fruits, use a traditional citrus reamer.

Finally, some recipes in this book call for ingredients to be muddled (pressed together in the bottom of a glass) which requires a muddler – a small stout rod made of wood, metal or acrylic (pictured above). Look for one without any paint or varnish coating on the crushing end, which could flake into your drink.

Some recipes in this book require you to muddle solid ingredients before building others on top of them. To do this, place the ingredients in your cocktail shaker or in the glass – make sure you are using a sturdy glass for muddled drinks, as fragile ones can break. Firmly, but not violently, press the muddler's crushing end against the solids, and repeat until they have broken down sufficiently to incorporate with the rest of your ingredients.

Shaking

To shake a drink, first build the ingredients in the appropriate part of the shaker – the smaller tin of a 'tin on tin' setup, the glass half of a classic Boston shaker or the bottom half of a three-piece cobbler shaker – then top with as much ice as you can fit. Seal the shaker with a firm, but not hard, tap. Pick up the shaker and move it firmly – but not too rapidly or violently – in a horizontal direction, back and forth, for at least 10 seconds. Open the shaker and strain the drink through both your Hawthorne strainer (or the cobbler's in-built strainer) and your fine mesh strainer, to capture any unwanted bits. This is called 'double-straining'.

All of the drinks in this book that contain egg will call for a 'dry shake'. To perform this, build the ingredients in the shaker as above, but shake the drink for around ten seconds *before* you add the ice. This allows the proteins in the egg white to uncoil and fluff up, creating a beautiful, pillowy texture. Once the drink is fluffed up, add your ice and shake again for at least ten seconds to properly chill and dilute the drink, then double-strain as you normally would.

Stirring

To stir a drink, build the ingredients in your mixing vessel of choice, then top with ice until the drink's surface is hidden beneath the cubes. Place your bar spoon (or a chopstick, in a pinch) between the ice and the wall of the glass, then gently rotate the spoon's stem around the wall of the glass by twisting it between your thumb and forefinger. The idea here is to push the ice *through* the drink rather than churning up the liquid and ice – the perfect cocktail stir is deadly quiet. To ensure that the drink is properly chilled and diluted, you'll need to stir for 30 to 45 seconds. Strain the drink through your Hawthorne strainer (or your julep strainer, if you're using one) and into the glass – unless you are using poor-quality ice, a second strain through a fine mesh strainer should be unnecessary.

Swizzling is a variation on stirring used in drinks made with crushed ice, where the aim is to churn the ice and drink together to chill and incorporate everything. Start by placing your wooden swizzle stick spoke-side down in the drink (or, if you are using a bar spoon with a flat disc on the end, disc-side down). Rub the shaft of the stick or spoon rapidly between your palms, and move your hands up and down to ensure the whole drink is churned. Keep swizzling until a frost forms on the exterior of the glass.

Glassware

Once you've made your drink, you'll need to serve it out of an appropriate vessel. While there's a dazzling array of glassware available, you only need a few different glass types for the cocktails in this collection: some stemmed coupe glasses (aka champagne saucers) for shaken and stirred drinks; tall, thin Collins glasses for carbonated drinks; and short, stout Old Fashioned (aka rocks) glasses for spirit-driven drinks served on the rocks. Specialty vessels such as v-shaped Martini glasses, bell-shaped Margarita glasses and copper mugs for Moscow Mules are nice, but by no means necessary. Second-hand stores are often a treasure-trove of cheap glassware, but make sure that your glasses will actually hold your drinks and any ice you want to

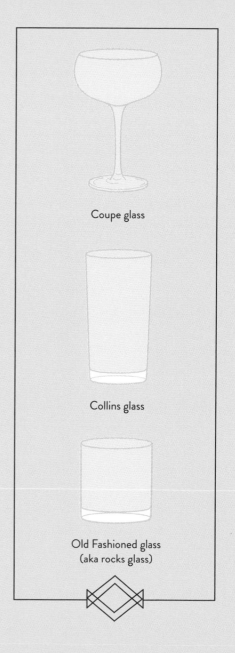

Coupe glass

Collins glass

Old Fashioned glass
(aka rocks glass)

put in them with some headroom to spare: look for coupes that carry at least 180 ml (6 fl oz), Collins glasses that carry at least 300 ml (10 fl oz) and Old Fashioned glasses that carry at least 360 ml (12 fl oz). Your cocktails will stay cool much longer if you chill your glasses before use – pop them in the fridge or freezer five minutes before you plan on drinking from them, or fill them with crushed ice and water for a few minutes.

Garnishes

Most of the garnishes featured in this book require no more work than popping onto a skewer and dropping into the drink (in the case of olives or maraschino cherries) or notching with a knife and balancing on the rim (lime wheels, pineapple slices, etc). One common garnish, however, takes a bit more effort: the citrus twist, which perfumes a drink with the oil from the fruit's peel. To make one of these, take the citrus fruit in question and slice a long swathe of peel from it, using either a knife or a vegetable peeler. You'll get more peel out of each fruit if you cut top to bottom, rather than around the fruit's circumference. Place the swathe cut side up on a chopping board and slice away as much white pith as you can, working your knife parallel to the board (don't scrape). You can neaten the edges of the peel at this stage if you like; if you want to be really fancy, use some pinking shears for a zigzag edge. Take the prepared swathe of peel and hold it, cut side up, over the drink. Gently squeeze the long edges between thumb and forefinger to release a mist of citrus oils over the surface of the drink. Wipe the rim of the glass – and the stem too, if you like – with the uncut, oily side of the peel, then give it a little twist to curl it and drop it into the drink. For drinks that feature an herbaceous garnish (usually mint), take a sprig of the herb and clap it gently to release some of its essential oils, so your guest can smell the garnish while sipping the drink.

Agua de Valencia may well be the bar world's most successful joke. It was invented in Valencia in 1959 as a lighthearted jab at a group of Basque travellers who frequented Valencia's Cervecería Madrid. This group would order the sparkling Spanish wine called cava by asking for *Agua de Bilbao* (Bilbao water), so called because natives of the Basque city of Bilbao had a reputation for knocking back cava as if it were water. Their bartender, Constante Gil, jokingly suggested that they instead try *Agua de Valencia* – and then had to quickly invent the drink.

Gil's quick thinking resulted in something like a turbocharged Mimosa: orange juice, vodka, gin and sugar lengthened with cava (presumably to please the Basque travellers). Anyone who has visited Valencia will understand why Gil reached for orange juice: the streets of the town are lined with decorative orange trees, and oranges are liberally festooned on the beautiful *azulejo* (painted ceramic) tiles that decorate city landmarks such as the main train station, Estación del Norte, and the main market, the Mercat Central. And, of course, the Valencia orange is named after Valencia – even though it is a Californian invention.

While the Agua de Valencia remained something of an off-list specialty at the Cervecería Madrid throughout the 1960s, by the 1970s it had spread to other bars and restaurants. With a revival of Valencian local identity and language after the death of Spanish dictator Francisco Franco in 1975, Agua de Valencia became a source of local pride and an icon of Valencian drinking culture. The boom in tourism to Valencia from the 1990s onwards can't have hurt the demand for this easy-drinking local specialty, either.

INGREDIENTS

45 ml (1½ fl oz) vodka
45 ml (1½ fl oz) gin
15 ml (½ fl oz) simple syrup
200 ml (6¾ fl oz) freshly squeezed
  orange juice, chilled
750 ml (25 fl oz) cava (or other dry or
  off-dry sparkling wine), chilled

METHOD

Build vodka, gin and simple syrup in a cocktail shaker. Add ice and shake well. Double-strain into a large jug. Add orange juice, then cava. Stir briefly and add fresh ice to jug. Serve in champagne flutes or coupe glasses.

BARTENDER'S TIP: The orange juice and cava should both be as cold as possible. The juice should be strained free of pulp and recently squeezed – an hour after squeezing, enzymes in the fruit will create a bitter flavour.

SERVES 5

AROUND THE WORLD
HONG KONG, CHINA

The trading posts of the world – places where cultures meet and goods are exchanged – have been the breeding grounds for any number of classic cocktails. So it's something of a mystery why Hong Kong, the world's gateway to China and one of the most important port cities in history, is responsible for ... well, no classic cocktails whatsoever. According to bar consultant Angus Winchester, the Pearl of the Orient can lay claim to being the birthplace of only one long-lived drink – the Gunner, a mixture of equal parts ginger beer and ginger ale with a dash of Angostura bitters. That's all well and good for cooling down on one of Hong Kong's notoriously sticky summer days, but hardly worth mentioning in the same breath as, say, the Manhattan (see page 80).

As if to make up for this embarrassing lack of classic cocktails, Hong Kong's current bar scene is a vibrant one, with any number of trendy watering holes creating original cocktails via cutting-edge methods. Hong Kong bars have a flair for unusual presentation: cocktails come in miniature porcelain bathtubs, complete with rubber duckie; in a blood bag, kept on ice in a kidney dish; and in a light bulb, to be decanted over a skull-shaped ice block. The Around the World punch from Hong Kong tiki bar Honi Honi doesn't buck this trend: it comes served in a halved globe. But with its clever mixture of Pacific tiki flavours (rum, passionfruit and pineapple), Asian floral notes (jasmine syrup) and out-and-out luxury (the bottle of Taittinger brut champagne on top), it also pays homage to Hong Kong's history and current role as one of the world's most powerful port cities.

INGREDIENTS

250 ml (8½ fl oz) pineapple juice
200 ml (7 fl oz) guava juice
150 ml (5 fl oz) cranberry juice
150 ml (5 fl oz) passionfruit purée
125 ml (4 fl oz) aged dark rum
100 ml (3½ fl oz) white rum
100 ml (3½ fl oz) golden rum
75 ml (2½ fl oz) lime juice
50 ml (1¾ fl oz) peach liqueur
22 ml (¾ fl oz) jasmine syrup
22 ml (¾ fl oz) banana syrup
5 dashes aromatic bitters
750 ml (25 fl oz) champagne (or other dry sparkling wine), chilled
passionfruit shells, to garnish
edible flowers, to garnish

METHOD

Mix all ingredients except champagne with ice in a large punchbowl. Top with champagne and stir briefly to incorporate. Garnish with passionfruit shells and edible flowers.

BARTENDER'S TIP: The original recipe calls for Taittinger brut champagne, but any dry sparkling wine will work in its place.

SERVES 10

BAMBOO

YOKOHAMA, JAPAN

The Bamboo cocktail has achieved a small measure of fame for being the first cocktail to be invented in Japan, but in many ways it's perhaps the *least* Japanese drink imaginable. The dry vermouth is French, the sherry Spanish and its inventor, bartender Louis Eppinger, German. A simple blend of two of the most popular products of the 1890s – sherry and vermouth – and a touch of bitters, the Bamboo is the kind of drink that could have emerged almost anywhere – in fact, versions of this blend appeared in America, and possibly in India, before it was supposedly first made by Eppinger in Yokohama.

The location of its birth might have been an accident, but it was a fortunate one. While the Bamboo doesn't *taste* particularly Japanese, it does possess a simple and functional elegance akin to the Japanese concept of *shibusa* – a word that expresses an artistic balance of simplicity and complexity, rusticity and sophistication, economy and quality. Many classic cocktails share this quality, which might go towards explaining why Japan so enthusiastically adopted cocktail culture and became the unlikely home-away-from-home for pre-Prohibition bartending techniques and standards during the latter half of the 20th century.

Like many other classic cocktail recipes, the Bamboo's template is incredibly flexible. If you are feeling adventurous you can mix different types of dry sherries to make a 'split base', such as a fresh manzanilla with a touch of nutty amontillado or palo cortado for depth – a nifty trick pioneered by Hidetsugu Ueno in Ginza's Bar High Five. You can swap out the dry vermouth for sweet white vermouth if you want something a little softer and less bracing (skip the simple syrup if you do this). But perhaps the most effective variation I've encountered (from French bartender Jean Lupoiu's 1928 book *370 Recettes de Cocktails*) is to replace the simple syrup with a splash of orange curaçao, which adds an extra hint of citrus and spice to what can be an otherwise forbiddingly austere cocktail.

INGREDIENTS

45 ml (1¼ fl oz) fino or manzanilla sherry
45 ml (1½ fl oz) dry vermouth
5 ml (¼ fl oz) simple syrup or orange
   curaçao (optional)
1 dash orange bitters
1 dash aromatic bitters
lemon peel, to garnish

METHOD

Stir all ingredients with ice in a mixing glass until chilled. Strain into a chilled coupe glass. Garnish with a twist of lemon peel.

BANANA DYNASTY

MAOTAI, CHINA

The world's bestselling spirit is one the average Westerner is unlikely to have tried, or even heard of: baijiu, a (mostly) sorghum-based distillate from China. Domestic demand is sufficient to soak up most of the 10.6 billion litres (2.8 billion gallons) produced annually, but a small amount makes its way out of China to reach Western palates. The taste can strike first-time baijiu drinkers as that of a stinky laundry hamper or rotten fruit. But what Westerners perceive as a strong funk is, in fact, a complex system of different fragrances (divided into 'honey', 'layered', 'light', 'rice', 'sauce' and 'thick') that Chinese aficionados use to judge and talk about baijiu.

Of the dizzying variety of baijiu styles available in China, the one Westerners are most likely to encounter is moutai, which is made in the town of Maotai in Guizhou province by the state-owned Kweichow Moutai company. (The town's name was changed from Moutai to Maotai after the 1949 revolution, to honour Mao Zedong.) Moutai is to baijiu as cognac is to brandy: the prestige variety, and the standard by which all others are implicitly judged. This fragrant and highly complex spirit is made from sticky sorghum that has been fermented with a traditional starter mould called *jiuqu*, then distilled nine times and aged for three years in ceramic pots. Richard Nixon famously partook of a few too many shots of it during his 1972 visit to China – something that must have endeared him to Chinese premier Zhou Enlai, as the visit was eventually hailed as a milestone in global diplomacy. When Chinese statesman Deng Xiaoping returned the favour and visited the United States two years later, Henry Kissinger said to him, 'I think if we drink enough moutai we can solve anything.'

Because moutai is a rare and mostly unknown ingredient, it isn't often called for in mixed drinks – something that the Kweichow Moutai company sought to change when they put on the world's first moutai cocktail competition in 2015. The winning entry, Banana Dynasty – created by Sydney bartender Bobby Carey – marries the earthy funkiness of moutai with fruit notes from banana liqueur, while vermouth and bitters bind these two opposing flavours into a harmonious whole.

INGREDIENTS

40 ml (1¼ fl oz) moutai
20 ml (¾ fl oz) banana liqueur
15 ml (½ fl oz) sweet red vermouth
2 dashes aromatic bitters
orange peel, to garnish

METHOD

Build ingredients in a mixing glass. Add ice and stir until chilled. Strain into an Old Fashioned glass and add a large chunk of ice. Garnish with a twist of orange peel.

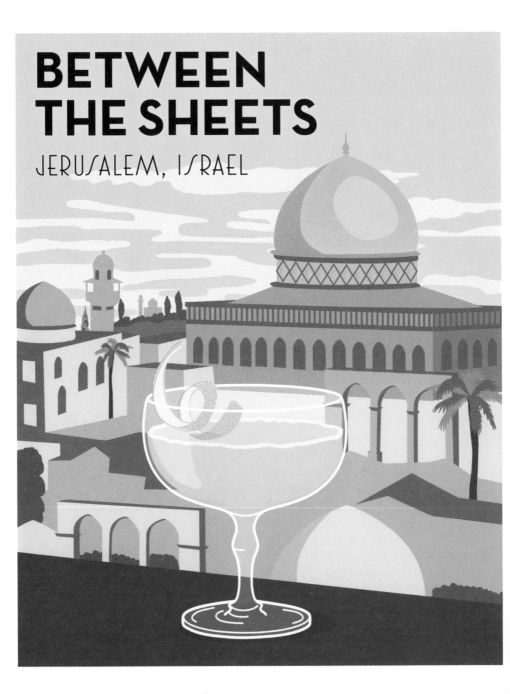

BETWEEN THE SHEETS

JERUSALEM, ISRAEL

In an age when a drink called the Red-Headed Slut not only exists but is well known in dive bars across the world, the name of this libation seems somewhat tame. But at the time the Between the Sheets cocktail emerged, its name would have seemed risqué indeed. The success of this cocktail might well be responsible for all subsequent mixological and linguistic crimes against taste such as Sex on the Beach and Screaming Orgasm.

Between the Sheets has an interesting pedigree. The traditional recipe is little more than a Sidecar (see page 134) with an extra splash of white rum – something that fortifies, but does not necessarily improve, that finely balanced classic. Others still are Sidecars sweetened with a touch of the strongly herbal French liqueur Bénédictine, tipping the drink into the realm of the dessert drink. Some claim that the cocktail can be traced back to Harry MacElhone of Harry's New York Bar in Paris (see page 49) in the 1930s, while others trace it back to one Mr Polly of London's Berkeley Hotel, where it was supposedly invented in 1921.

There's a third, much more interesting theory, with its own distinctive recipe. Charles H. Baker, the globetrotting drinks writer who chronicled the world's drinks in the 1920s and 1930s, recounts an afternoon spent in the bar of Jerusalem's King David Hotel, where he sought refuge from violence between Arabs and Jews roiling in the streets outside ('a nasty mess, with British Tommies in the streets finally, and machine guns and barbed wire entanglements – all the modern civilised show …'). He received a Between the Sheets from the bartender, Mr Weber, and was so taken with it that he got the recipe from Weber's own bar book, noting that it was 'already quite famous throughout the Near East'. Weber's version of the Between the Sheets calls for gin in place of the usual white rum, a small tweak that lends the drink a completely different character to the Sidecar – something a little spikier, with the sharpness of juniper cutting through the richness of the cognac.

INGREDIENTS

22 ml (¾ fl oz) cognac
22 ml (¾ fl oz) gin
22 ml (¾ fl oz) curaçao or triple sec
22 ml (¾ fl oz) lemon juice
lemon peel, to garnish

METHOD

Build ingredients in a cocktail shaker.
Add ice and shake thoroughly to chill.
Double-strain into a chilled coupe glass.
Garnish with a twist of lemon peel.

BIRD OF PARADISE
COLÓN, PANAMA

If you wanted to travel from America's east coast to join in the California gold rush of 1848 to 1855, one of the quickest routes was via Colón, Panama. The town had a reputation for squalor and lawlessness practically from the moment it came into being as the Atlantic terminus of the Panama Railroad, through which 'forty-niners' (gold-seekers) would pass on their way to California. The forty-niners brought their vices to Colón, which happily catered to them, creating Bottle Alley – an infamous stretch of mud where Americans consorted with prostitutes and got loaded. Local legend has it that when the alley was to be paved over in the 1890s, there was no need to lay a gravel foundation owing to the vast amounts of broken glass buried in the mud.

Colón had the fortune of being located on Limon Bay, where the long-planned Panama Canal would open up into the Atlantic. After several failed attempts by the French to construct the canal, the United States took over the project in 1904 – a move that led to Panamanian rebels declaring their independence from Colombia, and the creation of the American-administered Panama Canal Zone. The construction effort brought in boatloads of white Americans to perform the engineering and clerical work; the manual labour was, of course and unfortunately, reserved for poor immigrants from southern Europe and the West Indies. Enter the Stranger's Club – Colón's premier destination for expat Americans and the town's first proper cocktail bar.

One of the exotic libations whipped up at the Stranger's Club was the Bird of Paradise: essentially a New Orleans Fizz (now better known as a Ramos Gin Fizz) with raspberry syrup in place of sugar. This recipe, adapted from tiki historian Jeff 'Beachbum' Berry's book *Potions of the Caribbean*, is a refreshing drink to beat the equatorial heat – and with its ounce of cream and pink hue, it carries just a whiff of the tropical decadence and corruption for which Colón was once famed.

INGREDIENTS

60 ml (2 fl oz) gin
30 ml (1 fl oz) cream
30 ml (1 fl oz) lime juice
22 ml (¾ fl oz) raspberry syrup
2 or 3 dashes orange flower water
1 egg white
90 ml (3 fl oz) sparkling water
tropical flower, to garnish

METHOD

Combine all ingredients except sparkling water in a cocktail shaker. Dry shake to fluff up, then add ice and shake until chilled. Double-strain into a Collins glass and top with sparkling water. Add fresh ice. Garnish with a tropical flower.

BLACK RUSSIAN

BRUSSELS, BELGIUM

Poor old Belgium. Thanks to its long history of being fought over, partitioned and lorded over from elsewhere, it has a bit of a reputation as a mixed-up place, divided between three linguistic communities – French-speaking Walloons, Dutch-speaking Flemish and a small German minority – without a solid cultural identity of its own. Little wonder that Belgium is not only the home of the European Union, but also the butt of all of Europe's jokes. To add insult to injury, its best-known contribution to cocktail history has another country's name in it.

The first Black Russian was whipped up by Gustave Tops at Brussels's Hotel Metropole in 1949. Tops's creation was a twist on an existing cocktail, simply known as the Russian, which can be found in Harry Craddock's 1930 *Savoy Cocktail Book*. Its ingredients: equal parts gin, crème de cacao (white or black not specified) and vodka. The instructions for the drink indicate Craddock's opinion of this rather ghastly sounding combination: 'Shake well, strain into cocktail glass, and tossitoff quickski.' Tops's take on the Russian rather sensibly axed the gin and swapped out the crème de cacao for Kahlúa – a Mexican coffee liqueur that had debuted in 1936.

Tops's Black Russian really hit its stride in the early 1960s. Thanks to celebrity endorsements and some canny product placement in the James Bond films, vodka was the *geist* (spirit) that defined the zeitgeist, at least in the United States. Around the same time, Kahlúa was on its way to becoming the world's bestselling liqueur – courtesy of the marketing genius of importer Jules Berman, whose use of pre-Columbian figures in advertisements for the liqueur made canny use of the tiki craze (see page 79). The *Diner's Club Drinks Book* of 1961 introduced the prefix 'Black' to Tops's Russian, and a White Russian shortly followed, which eventually found pop culture fame as the favourite drink of Jeffrey 'The Dude' Lebowski. While the White Russian has eclipsed its progenitor's popularity, the Black Russian is a drink worth revisiting. When made with this relatively dry recipe, it's the kind of drink pouring that, like the Dude himself, abides.

INGREDIENTS

60 ml (2 fl oz) vodka
30 ml (1 fl oz) Kahlúa

METHOD

Build ingredients in a mixing glass.
Add ice and stir to chill. Strain into an
Old Fashioned glass and top with ice.

BARTENDER'S TIP: Make a White
Russian by pouring 30 ml (1 fl oz) of
cream over a bar spoon into the finished
Black Russian.

Scotch whisky has a reputation for being somewhat ornery in a cocktail. Part of this is due, no doubt, to the great diversity of flavours – if you make, say, a Rob Roy with a peaty Islay malt you'll end up with a very different drink to one made with a richer, sherry-finished Speyside. Consider too that for dedicated Scotch whisky drinkers, nothing could be more sacrilegious than adulterating their beloved *uisge-beatha* (water of life) with anything other than a few drops of water or, if you absolutely *must*, a cube of ice.

Alloway's great contribution to Scottish literature, 18th-century poet Robert Burns, was himself more than a little ornery. He could turn an elegant English sentence, yet called English 'the de'il's tongue' and preferred to write his poems in Scots dialect. He harboured Jacobite sympathies for the deposed Stuart royal family (even if pragmatism forced him to moderate their expression), yet became an enthusiastic supporter of the French and American revolutions, and looked forward to a time when workers would not have to 'labour to support/A haughty lordling's pride'. He worked as an exciseman, taxing the nascent Scotch whisky industry, yet satirised excisemen and wrote the famous line that 'Freedom an' whisky gang thegither!' Perhaps it's more than a little appropriate, then, that the cocktail named after him uses difficult-to-tame Scotch as its base.

The Bobby Burns as we know it is essentially a modified Rob Roy – itself a modified Manhattan (see page 80) with Scotch whisky in place of rye or bourbon. Just *how* the Rob Roy should be modified is a matter of some contention – the pre-Prohibition recipe outlined in the 1931 book *Old Waldorf Bar Days* skews the recipe away from vermouth and adds a dash of absinthe, while Harry Craddock's version from the 1930 *Savoy Cocktail Book* cleaves to a classic 50/50 Rob Roy base, but axes the orange bitters and dashes Bénédictine instead of absinthe. David Embury's *The Fine Art of Mixing Drinks* recommends the authentically Scottish Drambuie over French Bénédictine – but given the auld alliance between France and Scotland, and the role France played in nurturing Jacobitism, this recipe keeps the Bénédictine.

INGREDIENTS

60 ml (2 fl oz) Scotch whisky
30 ml (1 fl oz) sweet red vermouth
5 ml (¼ fl oz) Bénédictine
1 dash Peychaud's bitters
lemon peel, to garnish

METHOD

Build ingredients in a mixing glass. Add ice and stir to chill. Strain into a chilled coupe glass. Garnish with a twist of lemon peel.

BRANDY OLD FASHIONED

MILWAUKEE, USA

W hile French cognac has its devotees in craft cocktail circles, brandy's star has fallen in American mixology since the heady days of the 1850s and 1860s. Back then, a gentleman's Mint Julep (see page 90) was compounded with brandy rather than vulgar whiskey, and the cocktails at New Orleans's Sazerac Coffee House (see page 127) were whipped up with Sazerac du Forge et Fils cognac. These days, brandy no longer rules the roost – except in the state of Wisconsin. Here they mix a Brandy and Seven instead of a Seven and Seven, an order for a Manhattan will get you brandy mixed with vermouth, and an order for an Old Fashioned will get you a hefty dose of brandy charged with 'bug juice' (premixed sugar, bitters and water) and a splash of 7 Up, garnished with a half wheel of orange and a lurid red cherry.

This modern kind of Old Fashioned varies significantly from the Platonic ideal of the Old Fashioned: two ounces of spirit leavened with a hint of simple syrup and bitters, preferably served over one giant, glacial ice cube, garnished only with a twist of citrus peel. The Brandy Old Fashioned served in Milwaukee, Wisconsin is sweet, deceptively easy to drink, hopelessly kitsch in its choice of garnish, and retrograde in its construction methods. This recipe, by Portland bartender Jeffrey Morgenthaler, adds a touch of craft technique to the drink and tones down the sweetness, without compromising its Wisconsinite identity.

So why did brandy dominate the Badger State's drinking culture when all other states switched to whiskey at the end of the 19th century? According to Wisconsin-based restaurant critic Jerry Minnich, the German population of America discovered and fell in love with Korbel brandy at the 1893 Columbian Exposition in Chicago, Illinois – and Wisconsin was heavily populated by German immigrants. Curiously, the earliest print references to the Old Fashioned cocktail also come from Chicago, in the 1880s. Perhaps German visitors to the Columbian Exposition, enamoured with both Korbel brandy and the Old Fashioned, brought both back home to Milwaukee and combined them there?

INGREDIENTS

2 dashes aromatic bitters

1 sugar cube

½ orange wheel, thickly cut

1 high-quality preserved cherry

60 ml (2 fl oz) brandy
(preferably Korbel)

METHOD

Place all ingredients except brandy in an Old Fashioned glass. Muddle contents into a paste – but avoid crushing the bitter pith and peel of the orange. Add brandy and stir to incorporate. Top with crushed ice.

CAIPIRINHA

PARATY,
BRAZIL

Brazilians sure do like their cachaça, a sugarcane-based spirit similar to rum. Of the 1.2 billion litres (317 million gallons) of the stuff produced annually, only one per cent makes it out of the country – leaving just under 6 litres (1½ gallons) per year for every man, woman and child in Brazil to get through. And a huge portion of that cachaça gets consumed in the form of the Caipirinha, Brazil's national cocktail.

Despite the importance of the Caipirinha to Brazil's national psyche, the origins of the drink aren't exactly clear. A common story goes that it evolved from a mixture of lime juice, garlic, honey and cachaça – served hot – that was brewed up to ward off the effects of the Spanish flu epidemic that swept the world in 1918. With the garlic dropped and some ice added, the drink went on to experience national popularity after being the official drink at São Paulo's Modern Art Week in 1922. But recent evidence unearthed by Brazilian historian Diuner Melo suggests that the drink dates back to at least 1856, when a mixture of limes, sugar and cachaça was consumed in place of water during a cholera outbreak in Paraty, near Rio de Janeiro. Melo's argument is sound – booze was recommended during other cholera outbreaks of the 19th century (such as the outbreak in Inverness, Scotland, in 1832, which was treated with lashings of gin), and Paraty was once so closely associated with cachaça production that 'parati' is an archaic synonym for cachaça.

The idea of mixing cane distillate, lime and sugar isn't exactly new – it's a folk tradition across the Caribbean and South America that stretches back to the 16th century, when the first El Draque cocktail (see page 93) was whipped up to soothe British privateer Sir Francis Drake's upset tummy. Cachaça production in fact predates the modern rum industry in the Caribbean by a century – making cachaça one of rum's predecessor spirits. Perhaps it is appropriate, then, that the contemporary Caipirinha comes off as a kind of proto-Daiquiri (see page 30): the bashed chunks of lime floating in the murky liquid look akin to the black caiman that slither through the dark waters of the Amazon – something both primitive and deadly.

INGREDIENTS

½ lime
1 teaspoon unrefined
   brown sugar
60 ml (2 fl oz) cachaça

METHOD

Cut lime into small wedges. Place wedges and sugar at the base of an Old Fashioned glass. Muddle thoroughly to express the lime juice and dissolve the sugar. Add cachaça and stir to incorporate. Top with coarsely crushed ice.

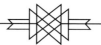

CHAMPAGNE À NICHOLAS II
ST PETERSBURG, RUSSIA

From the start of the 18th century until the Russian Empire's dissolution in 1917, the Russian nobility looked west for inspiration. In the case of St Petersburg and its founder, Peter the Great, 'looking west' was no mere figure of speech – St Petersburg was founded at the furthest western reaches of the Russian Empire, in territory acquired by Peter specifically for the purpose of access to the Baltic Sea. Peter's aim was to build a capital to rival the splendour of Versailles, laid out in a rational grid of broad, magnificent avenues. Because he was the Tsar of Russia, Peter could put an unusual amount of manpower into making that vision happen: over 100,000 serfs died during the construction of the city, and Peter forbade the building of stone dwellings outside of St Petersburg to ensure a steady supply of stonemasons. His successor, Catherine the Great, continued Peter's Francophilia (even though she herself was Prussian) by corresponding with the leading *philosophes* of the Enlightenment, including Voltaire.

Throughout the 19th century, France's leading champagne houses did a roaring trade in exporting the bubbly stuff to 'the Venice of the north', St Petersburg. Ever the intrepid capitalists, the Champenoise modified their product to suit local tastes. Observing that Russian drinkers kept bowls of sugar on the table to spike their wines, they started pre-dosing their champagne for the Russian market with large quantities of sugar: up to 300 grams (10½ oz) per litre, or almost three times as much sugar as is in modern Coca-Cola.

Given the Russian nobility's sweet tooth and Francophilia, it's perhaps not surprising that the last of the tsars, Nicholas II, liked a glass of bubbles and he liked it sweet. His own preferred method for sweetening his champagne was to add a splash of the French herbal liqueur Chartreuse, specifically the mellower, sweeter yellow variety. And while the global turmoil of World War I eventually spelled the end for Nicholas himself (who was executed, alongside his family, in 1918), it preserved a great deal of evidence about the drinking habits of the Russian nobility – excavated from the holds of merchant ships that were sunk to the bottom of the Baltic Sea, where the light, temperature and pressure combine to create near-perfect cellar conditions for champagne.

INGREDIENTS

10 ml (¼ fl oz) yellow Chartreuse
150 ml (5 fl oz) champagne (or other
   sparkling wine), chilled
lemon peel, to garnish

METHOD

Build ingredients in a champagne flute.
Garnish with a thin twist of lemon peel.

CHARLESTON

MADEIRA, PORTUGAL

I n 1419, when Portuguese explorer Infante Dom Henrique – known in English as Prince Henry the Navigator – discovered the uninhabited island of Madeira 500 kilometres (300 miles) west of the coast of Morocco, it was almost inevitable that it would be planted with grapes. Portugal had a long-established wine industry and even though Madeira's hot climate was better suited to sugarcane, its mountainous geography meant there were cooler spots in which grapes could flourish. Its early wines weren't worth writing home about – they spoiled quickly in the holds of the ships that took them from the island – but they proved much heartier after being stiffened with a dose of the local *aguardente de cana*, a local sugarcane spirit not unlike cachaça (see page 21).

Now that Madeira's wines were able to withstand a sea voyage, their consumers noticed something interesting – they got better the longer they were kept at sea. The heat and oxygen that would spoil other wines seemed to make madeira more delicious. The ingenious Madeirense figured out a way to replicate the effects of these long voyages: they would age the fortified wine in half-filled casks kept in hot attics, which would both heat and oxidise the wine.

Because madeira was practically immortal compared to other wines and because goods shipped from Madeira were exempt from British-imposed taxes, madeira became the tipple of choice of the American colonies, particularly in southern cities like Charleston, South Carolina. The founding fathers toasted the Declaration of Independence with it, and Francis Scott Key sipped on it as he composed what would eventually become 'The Star-Spangled Banner'.

Madeira's popularity has fallen drastically since its heyday. However, in recent years it has experienced a small renaissance both in the world of fine wine (where it has a reputation for excellent value) and as part of the craft cocktail movement's interest in heritage drinks. This elegantly simple recipe, from food writers Matt and Ted Lee, pays tribute to madeira's connection to the American South by pairing it with that other southern staple, bourbon whiskey.

INGREDIENTS

45 ml (1½ fl oz) dry or off-dry madeira (sercial or verdelho)
45 ml (1½ fl oz) bourbon whiskey
2 or 3 dashes aromatic bitters
orange peel, to garnish

METHOD

Build ingredients in a mixing glass. Add ice and stir to chill. Strain into a chilled coupe glass. Garnish with a twist of orange peel.

COFFEE COCKTAIL

VILA NOVA DE GAIA, PORTUGAL

England and Portugal have a long history of alliance. So when England went to war with France in the early 18th century, it was only natural that English merchants would look to Portugal for their wine needs. Thanks to very low duties on imported Portuguese wine, port wines from the Douro region became wildly popular in England. Soon enough the banks of the Douro river at Vila Nova de Gaia were studded with warehouses labelled with very English surnames such as Croft, Cockburn, Sandeman and Taylor.

The wines that were shipped out of the Douro were fortified to protect them from the rigours of the sea voyage to London. But, owing to growing demand, poor Douro wines were also adulterated with things like elderberries and sugar to improve their colour and flavour, giving Douro wines a bad reputation. By 1756 the Douro wine industry was in crisis, and the Portuguese prime minister of the time, the Marquês de Pombal, took control of the situation by setting up the world's first wine regulation body, the Companhia Geral da Agricultura das Vinhas do Alto Douro. Under its guidance, the wines of the Douro increased in quality and prestige. Douro winemakers started adding brandy early in the production process, thus preserving the grapes's natural sweetness. What we now think of as port wine was born.

The Companhia Geral suffered an unusual fate: its lodges were razed in 1833 during conflict between two contenders for the Portuguese throne. Over 20,000 pipes – around 1.1 million litres (290,000 gallons) – of port flowed into the Douro, turning the river purple. This setback for the industry was only temporary, though – heavily fortified, high-quality port had already become firmly established as the favoured tipple of England's upper classes. There is a small corpus of port-based classic cocktails, including this, the Coffee Cocktail, which famously doesn't contain coffee, but which (in the words of the anonymous editor who added it to the posthumous 1887 edition of Jerry Thomas's *Bar-Tender's Guide*) 'looks like coffee when it has been properly concocted, and hence probably its name'.

INGREDIENTS

1 egg
60 ml (2 fl oz) port
30 ml (1 fl oz) brandy
grated nutmeg, to garnish

METHOD

Break the egg into a cocktail shaker and remove any pieces of shell. Whisk lightly, then add remaining ingredients. Dry shake to fluff up, then add ice and shake until chilled. Double-strain into a chilled port glass or coupe glass. Garnish with freshly grated nutmeg.

CONDE NICCOLÒ

BUENOS AIRES, ARGENTINA

Argentineans love Fernet-Branca – actually, that might be putting it a little mildly. Argentineans love Fernet-Branca so much that the distillery in Buenos Aires that makes it for the South American market cranked out 4 million cases of the stuff in 2013, and is working on expanding production to twice that amount. They love it so much that a Fernando (a mixture of Fernet-Branca and Coca-Cola) is as commonplace a drink there as the humble Gin and Tonic (see page 54) is in England. They love it so much that in 2014 the Argentinean government added it to a price-freeze program to protect it from inflation. All of which would make sense if Fernet-Branca was Argentinean – but, in fact, it's Italian.

Fernet-Branca first arrived in Argentina in the late 19th century, alongside Italian immigrants who had picked up a taste for this profoundly bitter, herbaceous substance after its launch in Milan in 1845. Fernet-Branca was originally sold as medicine rather than a recreational drink – a veritable panacea, capable of easing menstrual pain, aiding digestion, diminishing anxiety, extinguishing headaches and counteracting the effects of old age. It was a strong booze laced with not-inconsiderable amounts of opiates (now reduced to trace amounts), which probably helped its popularity.

In the 1990s, the Argentinean branch of Fratelli Branca commenced an aggressive marketing push to young consumers to pair it with Coca-Cola in the Fernando. The popularity of the Fernando is now something of a double-edged sword for Fernet-Branca in Argentina – many drinkers now think that this spirit should only ever be mixed with cola. Speakeasy bar Harrison, in Buenos Aires, challenges this perception in the Conde Niccolò – a cocktail named after the current chairman of Fratelli Branca, Niccolò Branca.

INGREDIENTS

2 coin-sized slices of fresh ginger
60 ml (2 fl oz) Fernet-Branca
30 ml (1 fl oz) lime juice
30 ml (1 fl oz) cinnamon syrup (see tip)
ground cinnamon, to garnish
apple slice, to garnish

METHOD

Place the ginger in a cocktail shaker and muddle thoroughly. Add remaining ingredients and top off with ice. Shake thoroughly to chill. Double-strain into a chilled teacup (or Old Fashioned glass). Garnish with a sprinkle of ground cinnamon and an apple slice.

BARTENDER'S TIP: To make cinnamon syrup, dissolve 1 cup of sugar into 1 cup of hot water. Add 4 or 5 medium cinnamon sticks, broken up. Infuse in the refrigerator for 24 hours. Strain and decant into a sterilised container, and store in the refrigerator.

DAIQUIRI

DAIQUIRÍ,
CUBA

The Daiquiri – the original, that is, not any of its fruit-flavoured derivations – is almost the Platonic ideal of elegant simplicity. With just three ingredients, it seems like the easiest thing in the world to make – until, that is, you have to make one. Then you discover that this simplicity leaves any weaknesses in your bartending techniques with absolutely nowhere to hide. Figuring out how to balance the three elements of spirit, citrus and sugar begins to take on the difficulty of a medieval theologian's ontological argument for the existence of God.

Most histories of the Daiquiri credit its invention to American mining engineer Jennings Cox, who came to Cuba in 1896 to help the Spanish–American Iron Company exploit ore deposits in the Sierra Maestra mountains. In the town of Daiquirí, just outside of Santiago de Cuba, Cox blended the local Bacardí white rum with lime juice and sugar – a concoction that pleased junior medical officer Lucius W. Johnson. In 1909, Johnson took the recipe back to the Army and Navy Club in Washington, D.C., where it became a hit.

The Daiquiri was hardly an original idea, though, and it didn't take a *yanqui* (American) to come up with mixing sugarcane spirit, lime and sweetener. A very similar drink, the Canchánchara, was a popular beverage among Cuban rebels during the Spanish–American War of 1898 – the only difference being that the Canchánchara was not iced, and it was sweetened with *miel* (honey or raw cane juice).

It's fitting, then, that while an American 'invented' the Daiquiri, a Cuban perfected it. Constantino Ribalaigua Vert, head bartender of El Floridita in Havana, tested and perfected several variations of the classic Daiquiri. These variations – 'numbered like modernist paintings', as Jeff 'Beachbum' Berry puts it – included Daiquiri Number Four, which would go on to become Ernest Hemingway's drink of choice (see page 33), but if you want to test your bartending mettle, the original recipe is the way to go.

INGREDIENTS

60 ml (2 fl oz) white rum
22 ml (¾ fl oz) lime juice
10 ml (¼ fl oz) simple syrup
lime wedge or wheel, to garnish

METHOD

Build ingredients in a cocktail shaker. Add ice and shake thoroughly to chill. Double-strain into a chilled coupe glass. Garnish with a wedge or wheel of lime.

BARTENDER'S TIP: Just how much lime juice and sugar you will need depends on the acidity of the limes. Don't be afraid to tinker with the proportions.

DEATH IN THE AFTERNOON

PAMPLONA, SPAIN

When a young Ernest Hemingway first came to Pamplona, Spain in 1923, it was a charming but little-known backwater. Yet Pamplona's bullfighting festival, San Fermín, sparked a love affair between Hemingway and the town that powered two of his literary masterpieces: *The Sun Also Rises* and a nonfiction ode to bullfighting, *Death in the Afternoon*. These books would help turn Pamplona into the tourism powerhouse it is today.

As anyone who knows anything about Hemingway can tell you, the man liked a drink or two, and his creative talents extended to cocktail making – even if the resulting drinks were long on booze and short on balance. Hemingway's personal take on Constantino Ribalaigua Vert's Daiquiri Number Four (see page 31), with twice the rum and no sugar, lives on in contemporary bars as the Hemingway Daiquiri or Papa Doble. He also invented Death in the Afternoon, a drink of legendary potency named after his own book.

Hemingway's version, from the 1935 collection of drinks recipes by famous writers, *So Red the Nose, or Breath in the Afternoon*, calls for one jigger (45 ml/1½ fl oz) of absinthe, topped with enough champagne to attain 'the proper opalescent milkiness'. This doesn't sound so fearsome, until you realise that the absinthe Hemingway calls for could be up to 75 per cent alcohol by volume. Then comes Hemingway's wry little kicker at the conclusion of his instructions: 'Drink three to five of these slowly.'

It's perhaps unsurprising that, later in life, Hemingway was wracked by alcoholism, but he was also full of hatred for what he felt he had turned Pamplona into. In *The Dangerous Summer*, Hemingway wrote, 'I've written Pamplona once and for keeps. It is all there as it always was except forty thousand tourists have been added. There were not twenty tourists when I first went there nearly four decades ago.' Hemingway ended his days a tragic figure, eventually committing suicide in 1961, on the eve of San Fermín. One last, horrible twist to the story: he had two tickets to that year's festival in his desk drawer.

INGREDIENTS

45 ml (1½ fl oz) absinthe

120 ml (4 fl oz) sparkling wine

lemon peel, to garnish (optional)

METHOD

Pour absinthe into a chilled coupe glass or champagne flute. Slowly top with sparkling wine.

BARTENDER'S TIP: Garnish with a thin twist of lemon peel, or leave as unadorned as Hemingway's prose style – and drink with an abundance of caution.

DOCTOR

Swedish *punsch* – a liqueur traditionally served hot alongside yellow pea soup on Thursday nights – is about as Swedish as … well, nasi goreng. Swedish punsch is, in fact, based on the fearsomely brawny spirit Batavia arrack (see page 129), an Indonesian proto-rum made from molasses, red rice and palm wine. Swedish sailors developed a taste for punch made from Batavia arrack while plying the high seas in the early 18th century; by 1733, demand in Sweden was strong enough for the Swedish East India Company to begin importing arrack to the port town of Gothenburg. A warming bowl of hot arrack punch soon became a Swedish tradition.

The problem with arrack punch, though, is that it's a bit of a pain to prepare. You have to make an oleo-saccharum (a syrup of sugar dissolved in aromatic citrus oils; see page 43), juice lemons, add arrack and spices, and then combine the lot with hot water or tea. Wouldn't it be easier if there were a pre-mixed and bottled punch base of arrack, citrus, sugar and spices – just add hot water? Johan Cederlund, a wine and spirit merchant, started selling his own pre-mixed arrack punch base in 1845. Although this 'punsch' was intended to be lengthened with hot water, Swedes found they preferred it as a liqueur, often sipped cold and undiluted alongside coffee. By the 1850s, several competing brands of Cederlund's invention were being produced.

The popularity of this punsch liqueur didn't go unnoticed in the United States, and by the start of the 20th century it was being called for in a small number of different cocktails. But punsch's time came to an end in 1917, when the Swedish state monopolised the trade and distribution of alcohol through its Systembolaget, and many brands moved their production to Finland as a result. Prohibition followed. It would take later interest from tiki bartenders – particularly Trader Vic (see page 79) – to restore Swedish punsch to the American bartender's pantheon.

The Doctor cocktail first appears in Hugo Ensslin's 1916 book *Recipes for Mixed Drinks* as a simple blend of Swedish punsch and lime juice. This version, which incorporates improvements made by Trader Vic, is a little more complex and satisfying.

INGREDIENTS

45 ml (1½ fl oz) Swedish punsch
22 ml (¾ fl oz) dark rum
7 ml (¼ fl oz) lemon juice
7 ml (¼ fl oz) lime juice
7 ml (¼ fl oz) orange juice
lemon peel, to garnish

METHOD

Build ingredients in a cocktail shaker.
Add ice and shake thoroughly to chill.
Double-strain into a chilled coupe glass.
Garnish with a twist of lemon peel.

EAST INDIA

MUMBAI,
INDIA

W hile 17th-century England was the cocktail's birthplace, it most definitely grew up in 19th-century America, and concomitantly it was seen as something of a novelty in its mother country. The few early cocktails shaken up by British drinkers around the world had more misses than hits, although some of these mixologically unorthodox concoctions – such as the Singapore Sling (see page 136) and Pegu Club (see page 104) – have stuck around.

But British people weren't the only ones shaking up cocktails in the far-flung posts of the British Empire. Subjects who lived outside of England invented some – including the Singapore Sling, if the Raffles Hotel in Singapore is to be believed – while American bartenders invented others, often shipping them to the so-called American bars scattered throughout the Empire to lend them authenticity. For cocktail historian David Wondrich, the 'basic soundness' of its formula indicates that the East India cocktail was probably created by one of these early forerunners to the modern phenomenon of the travelling 'startender'. The drink's first appearance in print is no help in unravelling the mystery of who invented it: writer and bartender Harry Johnson, writing in 1882, merely notes that it is 'a great favourite with the English living in the different parts of East India'.

No matter who first whipped it up, or exactly where, the East India was a long-established favourite throughout the British Empire by the time travelling drinks scribe Charles H. Baker sailed into the Royal Bombay Yacht Club in what is now Mumbai, India, to sample a few in 1932. The recipe – basically a classic brandy cocktail made extra-suave with the addition of a few exotic sweeteners – hadn't changed much between Johnson's day and Baker's. When a drink is as well-constructed as this one, why mess with the formula?

INGREDIENTS

60 ml (2 fl oz) cognac

5 ml (¼ fl oz) curaçao

5 ml (¼ fl oz) pineapple gum syrup (see tip)

3 dashes aromatic or orange bitters

2 dashes maraschino liqueur

maraschino cherry, to garnish

METHOD

Build ingredients in a mixing glass. Add ice and stir to chill. Strain into a chilled coupe glass. Garnish with a maraschino cherry.

BARTENDER'S TIP: Peel and chop a pineapple into 2 cm (¾ in) cubes. Place in a bowl and cover with a simple syrup made of two parts sugar to one part water. Leave overnight, then strain and decant into a sterilised bottle. Store in the refrigerator.

EL MOROCCO

TANGIER, MOROCCO

When Charles H. Baker introduces the El Morocco cocktail in his 1939 book *The Gentleman's Companion*, he takes great pains to clear up its origins. 'El Morocco ... is a cocktail from North Africa, not any product of New York restaurants of similar name ... This is from the field notebook of a trusted friend on a Mediterranean cruise in 1938, and dated from Tangier, North Africa.' The need to spell this out would have been obvious to Baker's contemporaries. El Morocco wasn't only the name of the drink; it was also the name of the most famous nightclub in New York City to have emerged after the end of Prohibition.

The El Morocco nightclub began as a New York speakeasy in 1931, two years before the repeal of the Volstead Act. The club's transformation into the spot-to-be-seen was miraculous; as society writer Lucius Beebe put it in the club's own 1937 memento, *El Morocco's Family Album*, 'Given the entire antecedent social background of New York, it would still have been impossible to foresee the usurpation of the glitter scene of the most glittering city in the land by a single, and in itself, not overly resplendent hideaway in an entirely anonymous side street.' Hollywood stars Clark Gable, Kitty Carlisle Hart and Cary Grant were regulars, as were George Gershwin and Bing Crosby. With these high-profile customers came the cream of 1930s and 1940s society: the young Jacqueline Bouvier (later Jacqueline Kennedy, and then Jacqueline Onassis) made appearances at Elmo's, as it came to be known, as did both of her future husbands.

Part of the secret to the club's success was its canny development of three tools: the velvet rope, a strict hierarchy of table positions, and glamour photography. Readers of the society pages would know their favourite celebrities had been at El Morocco by the blue and white zebra-print banquettes, which popped in the black-and-white photographs of the time. With its unorthodox blend of cognac, port, and pineapple juice, this North African cocktail seems as surprising today as El Morocco's zebra print banquettes once were.

INGREDIENTS

30 ml (1 fl oz) cognac
30 ml (1 fl oz) pineapple juice
15 ml (½ fl oz) port (tawny, ruby or late-bottled vintage)
7 ml (¼ fl oz) curaçao or triple sec
7 ml (¼ fl oz) lime juice
5 ml (¼ fl oz) grenadine
pineapple slice, to garnish (optional)

METHOD

Build ingredients in a cocktail shaker. Add ice and shake thoroughly to chill. Double-strain into a chilled coupe glass. No garnish is necessary, but a slice of pineapple can be used if desired.

FALLING WATER

WELLINGTON, NEW ZEALAND

Feijoa trees are a common sight in New Zealand backyards, and every year during its short season the nation feasts on the fresh fruit (as well as feijoa jam, feijoa pie, feijoa chutney, feijoa salsa ...). The feijoa's guava-like fruit tastes similar to a combination of pineapple and banana, with a faint hint of mint and a certain intoxicating *je ne sais quoi*. Alas, the feijoa will never really become a commercial crop, despite its seductive and unusual flavour, because the fruit bruises easily and turns to mush a few days after falling from the tree.

Despite being something of a New Zealand icon, the feijoa is in fact native to the Río de la Plata region of South America. The plant became a popular ornamental tree across the world in the early 20th century, which is how it was introduced to New Zealand in 1908. Here it found ideal climate conditions for fruiting – and swiftly became part of the fabric of New Zealand life.

The feijoa's cultural status in New Zealand might explain why, shortly after entrepreneur Geoff Ross started making 42 Below vodka from his garage in Wellington, the company started work on a feijoa-flavoured vodka. The taste is not for everyone; as 42 Below rather forlornly says on its website about the feijoa flavour: 'Like Van Gogh before it, this little beauty has yet to receive the recognition it deserves'.

The Falling Water highball is a simple mixture of 42 Below Feijoa and Ch'i (a New Zealand–made, faintly herbaceous soft drink), garnished with a slice of cucumber. This cocktail came about when a (slightly tipsy) bartender from Wellington restaurant Matterhorn suggested that this feijoa vodka could work well with Ch'i and cucumber because all three ingredients are green (Ch'i comes in a green bottle, and the vodka bears a green label). The resulting highball possesses the same idiosyncratic allure as the fruit itself – and remains hugely popular at Matterhorn, which has become the world's number one buyer of 42 Below Feijoa.

INGREDIENTS

60 ml (2 fl oz) 42 Below Feijoa vodka

120 ml (4 fl oz) Ch'i

cucumber slice, to garnish

METHOD

Place vodka in a Collins glass and add Ch'i. Top with ice. Garnish with a long, thin slice of cucumber.

BARTENDER'S TIP: If you can't find Ch'i, it can be replaced with sparkling clear lemonade or a lemon-lime flavoured soft drink.

FISH HOUSE PUNCH

PHILADELPHIA, USA

The State in Schuylkill in Philadelphia – now known as the Schuylkill Fishing Company – claims to be the oldest continuously operating social club in the world, having been founded in 1738. George Washington dropped in for a visit in 1787, while he was presiding over the creation of the United States's Constitution.

He almost certainly would have been offered a glass or two of refreshing Fish House Punch, the club's official drink. This punch is a deceptively strong potion – so much so that Washington is said to have left his diary blank for three days following his visit.

Early print references to Fish House Punch are paeans to its strength and the quantities that the State in Schuylkill members regularly put away. William Black, in 1744, recalls being welcomed to Schuylkill 'with a Bowl of fine Lemon Punch big enough to have Swimmed half a dozen of young Geese'. By 1885 the club's official punch recipe was sufficiently well known that there was a piece of doggerel about its potency: 'There's a little place just out of town, / Where, if you go to lunch, / They'll make you forget your mother-in-law / With a drink called Fish-House Punch.' Yikes. As the State in Schuylkill fashioned itself as its own sovereign state, the club's members allegedly ignored the passage of the Volstead Act and continued to drink Fish House Punch throughout Prohibition.

This recipe, adapted from David Wondrich's book *Punch: The Delights (and Dangers) of the Flowing Bowl*, dates back to 1795 – not long after Washington's supposedly hangover-inducing visit to Schuylkill. It's still as delicious and dangerous today as it ever was.

INGREDIENTS

12 lemons
450 g (1 lb) sugar
700 ml (24 fl oz) lemon juice
700 ml (24 fl oz) dark rum
350 ml (12 fl oz) cognac
350 ml (12 fl oz) peach brandy
1 l (4 cups) chilled water
lemon wheels, to garnish
grated nutmeg, to garnish

METHOD

Prepare an oleo-saccharum – a syrup of sugar dissolved in aromatic citrus oils – by peeling 12 lemons in swathes (avoid the white pith, and keep the peeled lemons for juicing). Muddle the peels in the sugar until the sugar is wet with lemon oil. Let sit for an hour or more, then remove the lemon peels. Place the oleo-saccharum in a large punch bowl and add lemon juice. Stir to dissolve the sugar, then add dark rum, cognac and peach brandy. Dilute with the chilled water. Place a large block of solid ice in the punchbowl to keep its contents cool. Garnish each cup with wheels of lemon and grated nutmeg.

SERVES 10

FLAME OF
LOVE MARTINI
LOS ANGELES, USA

By the 1970s the Dry Martini had wandered a long way from its origins in the Martinez (see page 84). Gin was out, and vodka was in. The vermouth quotient, once so important to the drink, had been reduced so dramatically that it was practically a vestigial organ – the Martini's appendix, if you will. As for the bitters … forget about 'em.

Each of these permutations happened for a reason, of course. Vodka had become the spirit du jour in late 1940s America, and in the 1960s the Vodka Martini – shaken, not stirred – became a pop culture phenomenon thanks to the influence of James Bond. By 1975 vodka had become America's most popular spirit. Vermouth's decline can be linked to the devastating impact of both Prohibition and World War II. It didn't help that dry vermouth doesn't play particularly nicely with vodka. And orange bitters, once so essential to the Martini, were an extinct species by the close of Prohibition.

All of this meant that if you strolled into a hip bar in 1970s America and asked for a Martini, as Dean Martin was fond of doing, you'd get a cocktail very long on vodka and short on anything else. Little wonder, then, that after sinking a few Martinis at Chasen's, Beverly Hills's celebrity hotspot of the time, Martin asked his bartender, Pepe Ruiz, to come up with something new. Pepe's take on the Martini – a stirred vodka martini served in a sherry-rinsed glass – seems like nothing special, until you get to the garnish: a whole orange peel that is flamed over the glass. This loads the cocktail with aromatics from the caramelised orange oils, a not-too-shabby replacement for those missing orange bitters, and creates a show for the guest. Which might explain why Frank Sinatra was so enamoured with the Flame of Love that he bought 52 of them for his guests when his birthday party was held at Chasen's. After making just one of these, you'll feel sorry for Pepe.

INGREDIENTS

peel of 1 orange
60 ml (2 fl oz) vodka
5 ml (¼ fl oz) fino or manzanilla sherry

METHOD

Remove the peel from the orange in swathes. Build vodka and sherry in a mixing glass. Add ice and stir to chill. Take a chilled coupe or martini glass and flame all but one of the peel swathes by holding a match between the glass and the peel and squeezing the peel so the orange oils are directed towards the flame and the glass. Strain the cocktail into the glass, flame the last swathe of peel over the drink, and drop this last twist into the drink.

FOUR SEASONS GATHERING
CHIOS, GREECE

If asked to name a Greek spirit, most people would say ouzo. But ouzo, while very much Greek, isn't exactly unique. Anise-flavoured spirits are found all around the Mediterranean: Levantine arak, Armenian oghi, Turkish raki, Italian sambuca, French pastis and Spanish anís. For something completely Greek, look for mastiha: a spirit infused with the aromatic sap of the mastic tree, *Pistacia lentiscus*, which can only be gathered from trees grown on the tiny Greek island of Chios.

The mastic tree itself grows all over the Mediterranean, but only on the island of Chios (and on the nearby Çeşme peninsula in Turkey) does the right microclimate prevail for its sap to be harvested. Mastic producers make small incisions in the trees's bark, which then weep thick 'tears' of gum. These tears eventually fall to the ground – cleared in advance and coated in a layer of calcium carbonate – where they harden into nuggets, ready to be used. Herodotus mentions this traditional product in his *Histories* (written in 440 B.C.) as an embalming agent, and it was treasured around the Mediterranean as a breath-freshener and tooth-whitener. In many ways, it is the predecessor to today's chewing gum. Its value saw Chios become the plaything of empires; the Romans, Byzantines, Genoese and Ottomans each conquered Chios for its lucrative mastic gum trade.

Mastiha's unique flavour – both herbal and earthy, with notes of fresh mint, anise and carrot – makes it something of a challenge to mix in cocktails. Despite this difficulty, or perhaps because of it, mastiha has become a treasured component in the original cocktails being made in Athens's vibrant cocktail bar scene. This recipe, from Baba Au Rum's owner and manager, Thanos Prunarus, showcases the fresh herbal nature of mastiha by infusing it with lavender and deploying it in a citrusy sour.

INGREDIENTS

55 ml (1¾ fl oz) lavender-infused mastiha (see tip)
15 ml (½ fl oz) lemon juice
15 ml (½ fl oz) pink grapefruit juice
5 ml (¼ oz) maraschino liqueur
5 ml (¼ oz) vanilla syrup
2 dashes aromatic bitters
1 dash lavender bitters
grapefruit peel, to garnish
lavender sprig, to garnish

METHOD

Build ingredients in a cocktail shaker. Add ice and shake thoroughly to chill. Double-strain into a chilled coupe glass. Garnish with a twist of grapefruit peel and a sprig of lavender.

BARTENDER'S TIP: To make lavender-infused mastiha, infuse 1 teaspoon of dried lavender in 350 ml (12 fl oz) mastiha for 20 hours. Strain and decant into a sterilised bottle.

FRENCH 75

PARIS, FRANCE

A cannon called the French Canon de 75 modèle 1897 was a cutting-edge death-dealer when it was first presented at the Bastille Day celebrations of 1899. In fact, it was so cutting edge that the French military was still using it – with great effectiveness – 15 years later, at the outset of World War I. It could deliver up to 30 75-mm rounds per minute and, thanks to its hydro-pneumatic recoil, it didn't need to be re-aimed after firing. Given soldiers's fondness for drinking, it isn't surprising that the Canon de 75 modèle 1897 would lend its name to a cocktail with some 'kick' – say, a blend of calvados, gin, absinthe and grenadine. That, at least, is what is in bartending legend Harry MacElhone's 1919 book *ABC of Mixing Cocktails*, along with this note: 'This cocktail was very popular in France during the war, and named after the French light field gun'. It's a lovely, if quite boozy, drink – but miles away from what you'll get today if you walk into a decent bar and order a French 75.

The path from MacElhone's '75' Cocktail to today's French 75 is convoluted – add a bit of lemon, then take away the calvados, absinthe and grenadine, and replace them with champagne and sugar. Indeed, cocktail historians argue about whether MacElhone's '75' is at all related to the French 75 recipe that wound up in the 1930 *Savoy Cocktail Book* – and moved from there into bars around the world. Even so, as cocktail historian David Wondrich notes, the lemon-and-champagne version of the drink was hardly news even back in 1930: Charles Dickens, while staying in Chicago in 1867, used to entertain his guests with a 'Tom Gin and Champagne Cup' made of gin, citrus, sugar and champagne.

One last twist in the French 75's story comes courtesy of David Embury, whose 1948 *Fine Art of Mixing Drinks* calls for cognac in place of gin. He notes, 'Gin is sometimes used in place of cognac in this drink, but then, of course, it no longer should be called French'. While the cognac-based French 75 has its defenders to this day, and is delicious, this version clings to the only remnant of MacElhone's supposed original recipe by insisting on gin.

INGREDIENTS

60 ml (2 fl oz) gin

15 ml (½ fl oz) lemon juice

7 ml (¼ fl oz) simple syrup

60 ml (2 fl oz) champagne (or other dry sparkling wine), chilled

lemon peel, to garnish

METHOD

Build all ingredients except champagne in a cocktail shaker. Add ice and shake thoroughly to chill. Double-strain into a chilled Collins glass and add champagne. Top with fresh ice. Garnish with a twist of lemon peel.

FYNBOS
CAPE TOWN, SOUTH AFRICA

Africa's southern tip is home to the Cape Floristic Region, one of the world's richest biodiversity hotspots. This region is dominated by abundant *fynbos* (literally 'fine bush'), a generic term for small scrubby plants and bushes native to South Africa. The most well known of these species is one that you may have consumed: *Aspalathus linearis*, the plant from which rooibos tea is derived.

When Dutch colonists founded Cape Town in 1652, they discovered not only the Cape Floristic Region, but also wild 'grapes' (technically *Rhoicissus tomentosa*, a close relative), which showed that the land would be suitable for viticulture. By 1659 European *Vitis vinifera* cuttings were flourishing in the Western Cape, and the first South African wine was successfully produced. French Huguenots, driven out of France in 1685, brought with them viticultural knowledge and winemaking experience, while slaves from Java, Madagascar and Mozambique tended and harvested the vines.

The racism that powered the nascent South African wine industry in the 17th century would be its undoing in the 20th century. International trade sanctions against South Africa, designed to break the apartheid system, coupled with overproduction thanks to high-yielding grape varieties planted in the wake of phylloxera (see page 127), meant that South Africa suffered from a glut of grapes and not much demand for wine. In response, the powerful industry body Koöperatieve Wijnbouwers Vereniging (KWV) directed large quantities of these excess grapes to be distilled into inexpensive brandy.

South Africa's brandy industry was revived after apartheid and is now producing world-class stuff. This cocktail, adapted from the original invented by Johannesburg bartender Eugene Thompson, combines brandy with native rooibos tea to create a truly place-specific tipple.

INGREDIENTS

60 ml (2 fl oz) brandy (preferably South African)

30 ml (1 fl oz) rooibos-honey syrup (see tip)

15 ml (½ fl oz) ginger liqueur

2 dashes orange bitters

lemon peel, to garnish

METHOD

Build ingredients in a mixing glass. Add ice and stir until chilled. Strain into a chilled coupe glass. Garnish with a twist of lemon peel.

BARTENDER'S TIP: To make rooibos-honey syrup, mix two parts strong, freshly brewed rooibos tea with one part honey and stir until honey is dissolved. Decant into a sterilised bottle. Store in the refrigerator.

A typical version of the Gimlet's invention goes something like this: in 1867, Scotsman Lauchlan Rose patented a process to preserve lime juice without the use of alcohol, just before the 1867 Merchant Shipping Act was passed. This act declared that all British Navy ships had to carry stores of lime juice to ward off scurvy, and Rose's became the navy's lime juice of choice. Then, in 1879, a surgeon named Thomas Desmond Gimlette recommended that sailors mix their daily Rose's ration with a hefty splash of gin from Black Friars Distillery in Plymouth – overproof, of course, so that if it accidentally found its way into the ship's gunpowder the cannons could still be loaded and fired. The Gimlet was born, and British sailors's love of it led to Brits receiving the nickname 'limeys'.

It's a nice story, but it has more holes in it than the barrels of Plymouth gin that were supposedly leaking over the navy's gunpowder. First, citrus juices had been known for their scurvy-preventing properties long before Lauchlan Rose's birth – by 1755 a daily ration of citrus juice was mandated in Britain's Royal Navy. The 1867 Merchant Shipping Act? It actually required that the lime juice used by the Merchant Navy contain 'Fifteen per Centum of proper and palatable Proof Spirits' – which Rose's, being alcohol free, *didn't* have.

Perhaps all we can say with certainty is that the drink has a British naval background, and was probably first whipped up with Plymouth gin. The first recipe for a Gimlet proper, from iconic bartender and Scotsman Harry MacElhone's 1922 edition of *ABC of Mixing Cocktails*, notes that it is 'a very popular beverage in the Navy'. That recipe calls for a 50/50 blend of Rose's and Plymouth gin, ice optional. This recipe, however, opts for deliciousness over historical accuracy, and adds a splash of lime juice for freshness.

INGREDIENTS

45 ml (1½ fl oz) navy-strength gin
(preferably Plymouth: see tip)
22 ml (¾ fl oz) lime juice
22 ml (¾ fl oz) lime juice cordial (see tip)
lime wheel, to garnish

METHOD

Build ingredients in a cocktail shaker. Add ice and shake thoroughly to chill. Double strain into a chilled coupe glass. Garnish with a wheel of lime.

BARTENDER'S TIP: If you can't find high-quality navy-strength gin, use 60 ml (2 fl oz) of any dry gin. The quality of Rose's lime juice cordial varies depending on where it was produced – the version produced in the United States, for example, is a shadow of its former self. If you can't find a high-quality lime juice cordial, find a recipe to make your own at home.

GIN AND TONIC

KOLKATA, INDIA

London dry gin used to be a touch more disreputable than its fusty English image would suggest. In the late 17th century, when the British government imposed harsh tariffs against spirit imports and removed the monopoly held by the London Guild of Distillers, enterprising Londoners starting producing gin – a bastardised version of the Dutch genever (see page 63). Early London gin was produced on the cheap, often adulterated with turpentine and loaded with overbearing juniper flavour to mask its low quality. This wildly popular new spirit was soon linked with poverty, disease and crime. In 1727 author Daniel Defoe, of *Robinson Crusoe* fame, complained that 'the Distillers have found out a way to hit the palate of the Poor, by their new fashion'd compound waters call'd *Geneva*; so that the common People seem not to value the *French*-Brandy as usual, and even not to desire it'.

The passage of the 1751 Gin Act reined in the excesses of early 18th-century gin drinking, and gin embarked on the long, slow march to respectability. By 1858 – when the British Crown took command of the British East India Company's possessions in the subcontinent, creating the British Raj – gin was the favoured tipple of the English mercantile class. While the Crown was taking over the East India Company's administrative functions in their headquarters in Calcutta (now Kolkata), businessman Erasmus Bond was busy perfecting an 'improved aerated tonic water': a carbonated means of providing British colonists with their required daily dose of *cinchona* bark (harvested from a Peruvian tree that contains the antimalarial compound quinine). Mix this bubbly medicine with a stiff splash of gin and you have the classic Gin and Tonic.

While India may be the Gin and Tonic's birthplace, and England its spiritual home, it has reached its acme in Spain, where the Gintonic, as it is called, has become the nation's balm in economically troubled times. Many Spanish bars feature extensive menus of Gintonics, with each gin matched to a complementary specialty tonic water and garnished with suitably exotic flourishes.

INGREDIENTS

60 ml (2 fl oz) gin

120 ml (4 fl oz) high-quality tonic water, chilled

lemon or lime wedge, to garnish

fruit peel, rosemary sprig, juniper berries or spices, to garnish (optional)

METHOD

Build in either an Old Fashioned glass or a Spanish-style *copa de balon*. Gently add ice to fill. Garnish with a traditional lemon or lime wedge, or garnishes such as fresh fruit or peel, a sprig of rosemary, juniper berries or other spices.

The craft cocktail movement that has recently reinvigorated the world's drinking culture can list many achievements, but it is curiously lacking in drinks that can be called 'modern classics'. For drinks writer and bartender Jeffrey Morgenthaler, a cocktail must be well known, able to be made at most bars using common ingredients and techniques, and flexible enough to survive deliberate or accidental tinkering to be called a 'modern classic'. But the proliferation of house-made bitters and syrups, as well as the attention to detail that sees craft cocktail bartenders dial in their original recipes to precisely suit individual brands of spirits, has led to a kind of Balkanisation of the cocktail.

Fortunately for us, there are a handful of contemporary classics meeting that definition that have made the leap out from behind the wooden bars of their birth. New York City bartender Audrey Saunders, of Pegu Club fame, has created more than a few: the Old Cuban, Earl Grey MarTEAni and Gin-Gin Mule. So has the late Dick Bradsell: the Espresso Martini, Bramble and Treacle. Sam Ross's Penicillin is another, as is Paul Harrington's Jasmine. But for sheer economy of construction, few of these drinks can beat the Gin Basil Smash, created by Jorg Meyer for his Hamburg bar Le Lion in 2008.

The Gin Basil Smash is the kind of drink that could have been shaken up at any stage from the 1880s onwards – if only one of pioneering American bartender Jerry Thomas's protégés had thought to add a handful of fresh basil to a gin fix, that is. With only four ingredients and some very basic techniques – but more than enough flavour complexity – the Gin Basil Smash is a masterclass in elegant simplicity. Little wonder that it can now be found on cocktail menus all over the world.

INGREDIENTS

½ lemon
10 large basil leaves
60 ml (2 fl oz) gin
15 ml (½ fl oz) simple syrup
basil sprig, to garnish

METHOD

Chop lemon into chunky wedges. Muddle lemon wedges and basil leaves in the bottom of a cocktail shaker. Add remaining ingredients. Add ice, seal shaker and shake thoroughly until chilled. Double-strain into a chilled Old Fashioned glass. Top with fresh ice. Garnish with a sprig of basil.

BARTENDER'S TIP: For the best results, go for a lighter, more floral 'new world' style of gin. As the acidity and juiciness of lemons varies, you may need to add lemon juice or sugar syrup after shaking to correct the drink's balance.

top me if you've heard this one before. A man walks into a bar with a friend. The friend, named Biffy, is in a spot of bother, having promised his hand to one woman while harbouring affection for another. The man, Bertie Wooster, orders some drinks to calm both their rattled nerves. The drinks perform the expected magic, and as he is sipping his third, Bertie exclaims that 'if I ever marry and have a son, Green Swizzle Wooster is the name that will go down on the register, in memory of the day his father's life was saved at Wembley'.

The Green Swizzle can thank P.G. Wodehouse's short story 'The Rummy Affair of Old Biffy' for its literary immortality, but that immortality has been a double-edged sword as far as the drink itself is concerned. In fact, the Green Swizzle was, until recently, believed to be a mythical drink rather than an actual one.

Thanks to the historical research of author Darcy O'Neil, we now know that the Green Swizzle did indeed exist – and that what made the drink green was the addition of absinthe-like wormwood bitters. Sources from the late 1890s attribute the drink's birth to the Bridgetown Club in Barbados, from whence it spread rapidly throughout the Lesser Antilles. The recipe itself seems strangely mutable: as cocktail historian David Wondrich notes in *Imbibe!*, the only constants seem to be the wormwood bitters, spirits and cracked ice. The following recipe is Wondrich's own take on the Green Swizzle, utilising the very Bajan ingredient falernum – a spiced, rum-based lime liqueur.

INGREDIENTS

45 ml (1½ fl oz) base spirit of your choice: flavourful white rum, gin or old tom gin or genever
30 ml (1 fl oz) falernum
30 ml (1 fl oz) lime juice
5 ml (¼ fl oz) wormwood bitters (see tip)
60 ml (2 fl oz) sparkling water (optional)
Angostura bitters, to taste (optional)
mint sprig, to garnish

METHOD

Build base spirit, falernum, lime juice and wormwood bitters in a tall Collins glass. Top with finely crushed ice and swizzle with a wooden swizzle stick or bar spoon. Top with more crushed ice. If desired, add the sparkling water and bitters. Garnish with a sprig of lightly slapped mint and sip through a straw.

BARTENDER'S TIP: To make wormwood bitters, infuse 10 g (⅓ oz) dried wormwood and the thin-cut peel of one tangerine in 250 ml (8½ fl oz) overproof white rum or navy-strength gin for three days. Strain and decant into a sterilised bottle.

HANKY PANKY

LONDON, ENGLAND

During the dry years of Prohibition, the cocktail world's centre of gravity – once so firmly ensconced in the United States – shifted towards wetter climes. Well-heeled Americans would make the short leap to Cuba, where they discovered the delights of the Daiquiri (see page 30) and the Mojito (see page 92). Others found themselves further from home, in the cosmopolitan city of Paris (see page 49), or searching for drinks and the meaning of life and death in Spain (see page 33). But while these watering holes had their delights, it was to London that a great many of America's most talented bartenders and their customers repaired. And when they arrived, they encountered Ada 'Coley' Coleman – head bartender of the Savoy's famous American Bar, and the first female celebrity bartender.

Under the tutelage of the wine merchant at Claridge's hotel in London, Coleman had learned how to mix drinks – starting with the Manhattan circa 1899 (see page 80). From Claridge's she had moved to the newly renovated American Bar at the Savoy, and in a short amount of time became its head bartender. She worked at the Savoy for over 25 years, mixing drinks for the cream of Edwardian society, including the Prince of Wales, Charlie Chaplin, Mark Twain and the actor Charles Hawtrey.

According to Coleman, Hawtrey had a habit of dropping in to the American Bar after long days of work, and asking for 'something with a bit of punch in it'. After some experimentation, Coleman presented Hawtrey with an original cocktail – a mixture of gin and sweet vermouth spiked with a few dashes of potent Fernet-Branca bitters (see page 29). Hawtrey took a sip, then promptly drained the glass and shouted out, 'By Jove! That is the real hanky-panky!'

One of the bartenders fleeing Prohibition, Harry Craddock, took a job at the Savoy in 1921. At the end of 1925 the hotel shut the American Bar for renovation and retired Coleman. Craddock went on to author the famous *Savoy Cocktail Book*, which credited only one of its recipes to Coleman: the Hanky Panky.

INGREDIENTS

45 ml (1½ fl oz) gin

45 ml (1½ fl oz) sweet red vermouth

5 ml (¼ fl oz) Fernet-Branca

orange peel, to garnish

METHOD

Build ingredients in a mixing glass. Add ice and stir to chill. Strain into a chilled coupe glass. Garnish with a twist of orange peel.

HOLLAND FIZZ

SCHIEDAM, THE NETHERLANDS

I f gin is the queen of cocktail spirits – flavoursome, yet willing to mix with nearly everything – then genever is the spikier, less affable queen mother. With its malty heft and distinctly bready notes, genever doesn't taste very similar to contemporary London dry gins, and even less so to the lighter 'new western' style of gins – even though genever is the spirit that inspired gin. English soldiers had first discovered juniper-flavoured malt spirits while fighting alongside the Dutch in the Eighty Years War (1568–1648); a nip or two of this 'Dutch courage' helped steady the nerves before battle. When the Dutch William of Orange overthrew the British James II to become the king of England, Scotland and Ireland in 1689, Dutch genever became a fashionable drink, and Londoners soon began making their own imitation version, which they named 'gin'.

While English drinkers wholeheartedly embraced their homemade version of genever, drinkers in the newly independent United States much preferred the original. It was mostly produced in the Dutch port town of Schiedam, which remains the centre of the genever industry to this day. Genever was the spirit called for in early 'gin' cocktails from the 18th century, rather than the London dry style we know today.

Genever's dominance of the cocktail world began to ease in the late 19th century thanks to the taste for lighter cocktails, often modified with vermouth, which called for either old tom or London dry gin. *Jonge* genever, a lighter style stretched with neutral grain spirits that was born of necessity during World War I, became the standard in the Netherlands. But old-fashioned genevers – *oude* genevers and *korenwijns* – are now available worldwide. This recipe, a fizz adapted from iconic American bartender Jerry Thomas's 1873 edition of *Bar-Tender's Guide*, made 'silver' with additional egg white, is a great introduction to this heritage style of juniper spirits.

INGREDIENTS

60 ml (2 fl oz) genever (oude genever or korenwijn)
15 ml (½ fl oz) lemon juice
7 ml (¼ fl oz) simple syrup
1 egg white
60 ml (2 fl oz) sparkling water
lemon peel, to garnish (optional)
mint sprig, to garnish (optional)

METHOD

Combine all ingredients except sparkling water in a cocktail shaker. Dry shake to fluff up, then add ice and shake until chilled. Add sparkling water to a Collins glass and slowly double-strain the shaker's contents over the sparkling water. Add fresh ice, if desired. Garnish with a twist of lemon peel or a sprig of lightly slapped mint.

IRISH COFFEE

FOYNES, IRELAND

Airport bars and restaurants are almost without exception dismal places – then again, the world of aviation is a very different place now to the world of aviation back in 1943. At that time, transatlantic passenger flights were a novelty and certainly not within most people's budget. Flights were conducted by flying boats, as there were no land runways large enough to accommodate the planes required for such a crossing. Foynes, on the west coast of Ireland, with its calm harbour and a railway link to Limerick and beyond, was the natural candidate for the European terminal for transatlantic seaplane flights.

The well-heeled of the time had certain expectations of luxury, so in 1943 the Irish government appointed Dr Brendan O'Regan, a successful hotelier, as the Catering Comptroller at Foynes flying boat base. His chef, Joe Sheridan, created the Irish Coffee in the winter of that same year as a warming beverage to give to passengers whose seaplane had been turned around on the passage to Newfoundland. It was essentially a hot cup of coffee spiked with some Irish whiskey, smoothed out with sugar and with a rich float of cream on top. After some tinkering – including placing the drink in a more attractive stemmed glass – the Irish Coffee was ready for prime time. Sadly for Foynes, though, the drink was perfected not long before the nearby Shannon airport became ready for transatlantic flights, and both Sheridan and Irish Coffee shortly decamped there.

While the drink was invented in Foynes, it became famous thanks to San Francisco's Buena Vista Cafe. Stanton Delaplane, a travel writer for the *San Francisco Chronicle*, first tried the Irish Coffee during a layover at the Shannon airport in 1952. On his return to San Francisco, Delaplane convinced the owners of the Buena Vista to replicate the drink – and, after some experimentation, they managed to nail it. The Buena Vista is now renowned for its Irish Coffees, and serves thousands per day.

INGREDIENTS

45 ml (1½ fl oz) Irish whiskey
22 ml (¾ fl oz) simple syrup
120 ml (4 fl oz) hot filter coffee
whipped thickened (heavy) cream

METHOD

Heat a stemmed Irish coffee glass with piping hot water. Discard hot water. Build all ingredients except whipped cream in glass. Stir briefly. Gently float whipped cream on drink.

BARTENDER'S TIP: The coffee should be very hot and very fresh, and the cream whipped by hand until it is just under stiff. The completed drink should resemble a pint of Guinness.

65

JÄGERITA
WOLFENBÜTTEL, GERMANY

If you had asked a liquor industry consultant circa 1984 what the next big thing in American drinking would be, it's unlikely they would have said Jägermeister – a herbal liqueur invented in Wolfenbüttel, Germany, in 1934. Even if they had heard of it, it wouldn't have seemed like a good candidate for success: a dark brown, syrupy potion, loaded with bitter herbs, and with a whiff of Nazi history about it (Hermann Göring was a fan). It needed a marketing genius named Sidney Frank to make Jägermeister what it is today – the party-starting shot of choice across the world.

Frank acquired the rights to import Jägermeister to the United States in 1973, but it took college students at Louisiana State University's Baton Rouge and New Orleans campuses to make Frank see the potential in the product. In 1985, for reasons opaque, these students developed a taste for the stuff, leading to a puff piece about the fad in the Baton Rouge *Advocate* (the quoted students called Jägermeister 'liquid Valium' and claimed it had aphrodisiac properties). Frank, sensing an opportunity, quickly assembled a team of attractive 'Jägerettes' to hand out copies of the article to bars in the area, and hastily put up eight ironic billboards featuring a wincing man and the tagline 'so smooth'. Frank swiftly leveraged the drink's popularity in Louisiana to make it the de facto drink for party time.

Jägermeister's popularity with the hard-partying fraternity set has been both a blessing for the company (in terms of its income) and a curse (in terms of its perception). Renowned not for its complexity as a digestif but as something to bomb into Red Bull, Jägermeister was, until recently, black-listed from the more self-serious craft cocktail joints. One of the drinks that has helped to rehabilitate Jägermeister's reputation is the Jägerita, a simple-but-effective twist on the Margarita (see page 82). Invented by Argentinean bartender David Cordoba in 2008 and passed around as something of a bartender's secret, the drink became better known thanks to Portland, Oregon, bartender Jeffrey Morgenthaler, who has served as its public champion.

INGREDIENTS

45 ml (1½ fl oz) Jägermeister
22 ml (¾ fl oz) curaçao or triple sec
22 ml (¾ fl oz) lime juice
15 ml (½ fl oz) simple syrup
lime wheel, to garnish

METHOD

Build ingredients in a cocktail shaker. Add ice and shake thoroughly to chill. Double-strain into a chilled coupe glass. Garnish by placing a lime wheel to float in the drink.

JAPANESE SLIPPER

MELBOURNE, AUSTRALIA

Outside of Australia, the Japanese Slipper is regarded – if indeed it is known at all – as a curiosity: a small and perhaps regrettable footnote in the history of 1980s drinks. And while its popularity in its home country has definitely fallen, the Japanese Slipper still looms large in Australian drinkers imaginations – either as a reviled symbol of the excesses of the 1980s and 1990s, or as a nostalgic memory of a more innocent, pre-internet time when Australian mixology wasn't quite so self-serious.

First concocted in 1984 by Jean-Paul Bourguignon at Mietta's restaurant in the Melbourne suburb of North Fitzroy, the Japanese Slipper would eventually pop up on cocktail lists the world over. Part of its appeal, no doubt, is the ease of remembering its recipe – it consists of three ingredients in equal parts. It also uses what was, in the early 1980s, a very trendy product: Midori, a neon-green, melon-flavoured liqueur produced by Japanese distiller Suntory. Midori had been launched at a star-studded party at New York City's Studio 54 in 1978, the year after *Saturday Night Fever* had cemented disco's dominance over American pop culture, and it survived the disco backlash to become a back-bar staple of the 1980s. The fact that Bourguignon was working at Mietta's – in 1984 a rapidly ascending star of Melbourne's fine-dining scene – meant that his drink would have been seen and emulated by his peers.

The Japanese Slipper, with its heady rush of sugar and lurid colour, quickly became the go-to cocktail for the Australian casual drinker. It would retain that position until the middle of the 2000s, when it was deposed by the almighty Espresso Martini – the London-born cocktail invented by the late (and great) Dick Bradsell that eventually found its spiritual home in coffee-loving Melbourne. The Japanese Slipper now lives on as an International Bar Association official cocktail and can still be found in suburban pubs and clubs throughout Australia.

INGREDIENTS

30 ml (1 fl oz) Midori
30 ml (1 fl oz) Cointreau
30 ml (1 fl oz) lemon juice
maraschino cherry, to garnish

METHOD

Build ingredients in a cocktail shaker. Add ice and shake thoroughly to chill. Double-strain into a chilled coupe glass. Garnish with a maraschino cherry.

BARTENDER'S TIP: The Japanese Slipper's balance relies on the use of Cointreau rather than a generic triple sec. Cointreau is drier and, at 40 per cent alcohol by volume, significantly stronger than most other triple secs.

JUNGLE BIRD
KUALA LUMPUR, MALAYSIA

ost cocktails come from an easily identifiable lineage, or form part of a broader family of drinks. But there are a few freaks and outliers – drinks that appear to have emerged in a class of their own, with strange liquor combinations and odd proportions that, bizarrely, just *work* – and the Jungle Bird is one of these.

The Jungle Bird's origin is shrouded in mystery, but it is apparently the creation of an unknown bartender from the now-defunct Aviary bar at Kuala Lumpur's Hilton hotel in 1978. The drink might have disappeared into cocktail oblivion were it not for writer and tiki drink enthusiast Jeff 'Beachbum' Berry, who spotted a recipe for it in John J. Poister's 1989 book *The New American Bartender's Guide*. Berry included the recipe in his 2002 *Beachbum Berry's Intoxica!*, and the Jungle Bird took flight from there, eventually landing (after a few recipe tweaks) on cocktail lists across the world.

Although the combination of ingredients might seem odd at first glance – dark rum, pineapple juice, lime, simple syrup and … Campari? – once you've had a sip, it's easy to understand the Jungle Bird's appeal to bartenders. It forms something of a bridge between the gaudy, hedonistic world of tropical tiki drinks and the amaro-loving world of the craft cocktail revival. The dark rum makes the drink pleasantly complex (for best results, use a brand heavy on molasses flavour, such as Cruzan Backstrap), while the Campari balances it with some bracing bitterness. With just five relatively common ingredients – positively minimalist by tiki standards – it's the kind of drink that nearly any bar in the world can make, and it's also perfect for making at home.

INGREDIENTS

45 ml (1½ fl oz) dark rum
45 ml (1½ fl oz) pineapple juice
22 ml (¾ fl oz) Campari
15 ml (½ fl oz) lime juice
15 ml (½ fl oz) simple syrup
orange wedge, to garnish (optional)
pineapple fronds, to garnish (optional)
pineapple wedge, to garnish (optional)

METHOD

Build ingredients in a cocktail shaker. Add ice, shake and strain into an Old Fashioned glass. Top with a chunk of ice or ice cubes. Garnish with a wedge of orange or pineapple on the rim of the glass, or pop in a few pineapple fronds.

BARTENDER'S TIP: Make the garnish as elaborate as you like – this is tiki, after all. Fresh edible flowers work well, as do maraschino cherries wrapped in orange wheels and skewered.

KIR DIJON, FRANCE

I f you're flipping through this book looking for something easy to put together that is nonetheless delicious – well, stop here. The Kir contains just two ingredients, it's mixed in the glass it is served in, and you don't even need any ice or a garnish. It's also sneakily sophisticated, and exudes a Gallic chic that will transport you to the cafe terraces of Paris (where, unlike most other cocktails, the Kir is firmly woven into everyday life). Perhaps best of all, it has a fascinating backstory.

The Kir is named after Canon Félix Kir, a man who trained as a priest, became a French resistance hero in World War II, and then found his calling as a politician. In his sixties, when Nazi Germany invaded France, he distinguished himself with acts of resistance against the collaborationist Vichy regime. He helped 5000 French POWs escape from the Longvic camp, and was twice sentenced to death by firing squad, but managed to leverage his position as a priest to avoid execution. He returned to Dijon on the day of its liberation (11 September 1944) as a hero, was made a knight of the Legion of Honour in 1946, and served the rest of his life as Dijon's mayor.

As mayor of Dijon and a veteran of two wars, Kir had a keen interest in what the French call *jumelage* (twinning) – the practice of pairing towns in different countries to promote cross-cultural understanding, with the hope of preventing future wars. Under Kir's mayorship, Dijon started twinning with towns and cities across the world – starting with former enemy Mainz, Germany, in 1958, and eventually twinning with nine others. This low-level diplomatic work required a lot of hosting, and Kir would entertain his official guests with a glass of blanc-cassis – a traditional Burgundian mixture of the bracingly austere local white wine made from the aligoté grape, softened by another local product, crème de cassis (blackcurrant liqueur). Prior to the war, aligoté was hardly the pride of Burgundy, which had world-famous grands crus (made from pinot noir and chardonnay) – but much of the good stuff had been plundered from Burgundy's cellars during the war. Kir's championing of the blanc-cassis turned it into a global sensation in the 1950s and 1960s, which helped the Burgundian wine industry recover from the war. Little wonder, then, that the drink is now named after him.

INGREDIENTS

150 ml (5 fl oz) dry white wine, chilled
15 ml (½ fl oz) crème de cassis

METHOD

Build ingredients in a wine glass. Stir briefly to incorporate. Serve without a garnish.

LAST WORD
DETROIT, USA

The Last Word is, to purloin Winston Churchill's famous phrase, 'a riddle, wrapped in a mystery, inside an enigma'. Let's start with the recipe, which gives equal weight to gin, lime juice, and two piquant liqueurs: green Chartreuse and maraschino. 'There are few wilder-looking mixtures in the annals of classic barkeeping', writes David Wondrich in *Imbibe!*, 'but somehow it just works'. This is probably down to both the pungency and potency of its two liqueurs – at 55 and 38 per cent alcohol by volume, respectively, they more than make up for the relatively small pour of gin, and both gin and lime act as a bridge between their two bold, assertive flavour profiles.

Mystery solved. But why did such a refined and delicious drink lie in obscurity for so long? Well, its historical origins are a little tangled. The drink first appears in print in Ted Saucier's 1951 book *Bottoms Up*, which says, 'This cocktail was introduced around here about thirty years ago by Frank Fogarty, who was very well known in vaudeville'. A little maths leads the reader to conclude that the drink was invented in 1921 – right in the thick of Prohibition. Ergo the oft-repeated claim that the drink was invented by Frank Fogarty at the Detroit Athletic Club during Prohibition. But a recently found menu from July 1916 that bears the drink's name dates from before Fogarty's first visit to the Detroit Athletic Club in December 1916, which means that Fogarty picked the drink up from the club, not the other way around. Bearing in mind that Saucier was a New Yorker and that *Bottoms Up* is an impressive tome that would have taken years to put together, it becomes clear: the 'here' is New York, and 'around thirty years ago' could have been written before 1948. Fogarty deserves credit not for inventing the drink, then, but for passing it on to the Waldorf-Astoria bar team.

More credit where credit is due: while the drink's origins remain misty, it was very evidently popularised by legendary Seattle bartender Murray Stenson, who began serving it at the Zig Zag Café in the early 2000s. It soon became a standard-bearer for the craft approach to cocktails: spirit-driven, historically minded and (most importantly) utterly delicious.

INGREDIENTS

22 ml (¾ fl oz) gin
22 ml (¾ fl oz) green Chartreuse
22 ml (¾ fl oz) maraschino liqueur
  (preferably Luxardo)
22 ml (¾ fl oz) lime juice
lime peel, to garnish

METHOD

Build ingredients in a cocktail shaker. Add ice, shake thoroughly to chill and strain into a chilled coupe glass. Garnish with a twist of lime peel.

Bolivia is famous for its elevations: El Alto airport is the world's highest international airport, Lake Titicaca is the world's highest navigable lake and La Paz is the world's highest capital city (depending on how you define the term 'capital city' – Bolivia has two). In La Paz, the wealthiest neighbourhoods don't have the best views – they are located at the lowest points of the city, where the air is richer in oxygen. And it's thanks to Bolivia's sometimes unforgiving altitudes that the national spirit, singani, has such a unique flavour.

Like pisco (see page 109), singani is a clear, unaged grape-based spirit. But Bolivia's altitude makes singani a little different: the boiling point of ethanol is lower in high elevations, which means less heat is required to distil singani. This means that more of the grape's aromatics are kept intact – and since singani is made from the notoriously aromatic Muscat of Alexandria grapes, the resulting spirit offers a bouquet of floral grape characteristics.

Singani's unique flavour profile – light, floral and complex – makes it a natural team player in cocktails, and it can replace gin, pisco, tequila or light rums with ease. It forms the basis of the cocktail list at Gustu, the La Paz restaurant owned by Danish chef Claus Meyer that serves meals and drinks made from exclusively Bolivian ingredients. The Llajua – a tangy, slightly savoury cocktail – is made using the excess liquid from preparing the restaurant's *llajua* (spicy Bolivian salsa). This version swaps in a spicy tomato and locote chilli shrub.

INGREDIENTS

60 ml (2 fl oz) singani
30 ml (1 fl oz) tomato and locote chilli shrub (see tip)
15 ml (½ fl oz) lime juice
cherry tomatoes, to garnish

METHOD

Build ingredients in a cocktail shaker. Add ice and shake thoroughly to chill. Double-strain into an Old Fashioned glass. Top with ice. Garnish with cherry tomatoes.

BARTENDER'S TIP: To make the shrub, place 1 cup white vinegar in a clean container with ½ ripe banana, sliced. In a separate bowl, place 2 cups chopped ripe tomatoes, 2 finely diced Bolivian locote chillies (or 2 small red chillies) and a handful of finely chopped *quirquiña* or a mixture of coriander (cilantro), rocket (arugula) and mint and 1 cup white sugar. Mix well and cover. Leave both the sugar and vinegar mixtures in the refrigerator overnight to infuse. Strain liquids from both sugar and vinegar mixtures, lightly pressing the solids to extract all liquid. Combine both liquids and whisk to incorporate. Store the shrub in a sterilised glass bottle in the refrigerator.

MAI TAI
TAHITI, FRENCH POLYNESIA

L iteral-minded readers are probably already composing their angry emails: 'Don't you know that Trader Vic invented the Mai Tai in Oakland, California?' Well – yes. But does the Mai Tai *belong* to Oakland, California, in any meaningful sense? Not a chance. The Mai Tai was born out of a sense of escape from quotidian places like Oakland. After the experience of World War II's Pacific theatre, middle-class white Americans developed a nostalgic taste for the exoticism of Pasifika culture – despite the fact that, more often that not, they got the details wrong. They would come to indulge that taste and slake their thirsts at soon-to-be-iconic tiki bars such as Don's Beachcomber and Trader Vic's.

Tiki titans Ernest Raymond Beaumont Gantt (aka Don the Beachcomber) and Victor Jules Bergeron, Jr (aka Trader Vic) had a long history of friendly rivalry. Gantt was the first to open a tiki bar, throwing the doors open to Don's Beachcomber Cafe in Hollywood, California, in 1933. Despite the effects of the Great Depression, it was an instant hit with celebrities. Not long after, Bergeron opened the eskimo-themed bar Hinky Dinks in Oakland, California. Looking around for something that would give him an edge, he found Gantt's bar and copied the concept. Trader Vic's would become the most successful tiki bar chain of the post-World War II era.

Gantt claimed that he invented the Mai Tai in 1933, and there is certainly a passing resemblance between the Mai Tai and Gantt's own Q.B. Cooler. But the version of the drink that became a worldwide sensation is inarguably the one that Bergeron claimed to have invented in 1944 at Trader Vic's – rum, lime juice, rock candy syrup, curaçao and a sweet almond syrup called orgeat.

When made according to Bergeron's recipe (with a tweak courtesy of Jeff 'Beachbum' Berry, who replaces the original Wray and Nephew 17-year-old rum with a blend of two rums), you can see why Carrie Guild, the first customer to have sipped it, exclaimed 'Maita'i roa ae!' – 'Out of this world!'

INGREDIENTS

30 ml (1 fl oz) dark Jamaican rum
30 ml (1 fl oz) aged Martinique rhum agricole
30 ml (1 fl oz) lime juice
15 ml (½ fl oz) orange curaçao
15 ml (½ fl oz) orgeat
7 ml (¼ fl oz) simple syrup
mint sprig, to garnish
edible flower, to garnish

METHOD

Combine all ingredients in a cocktail shaker. Add ice and shake thoroughly to chill. Strain into an Old Fashioned glass and top with crushed ice. Garnish with a sprig of mint and an edible flower.

Forget the story you may have heard about Winston Churchill's mother, Jennie Jerome, inventing the Manhattan in order to celebrate Samuel Tilden's election as governor of New York. It turns out that she was back home in Oxfordshire giving birth to the future prime minister and wartime hero of England at the time she was reportedly mixing rye and vermouth in the Big Apple. The truth, unfortunately, is more prosaic: we don't know exactly who invented the Manhattan. David Wondrich's *Imbibe!* lists two compelling candidates: George Black, who ran a saloon named the Manhattan Inn, or 'some anonymous genius' at the Manhattan Club. In either case the drink would have first arisen in the late 1860s or early 1870s; by the 1880s, it had become the toast of the town.

It's not hard to see why it was popular: by adding vermouth to the Whiskey Cocktail (the predecessor to what we know as the Old Fashioned), whoever invented the Manhattan created something more sophisticated. No longer packing the same punch, this new drink split the difference between the world of boozy cocktails and more effete drinks such as the Vermouth Cocktail (basically chilled vermouth with a dash of bitters). It opened up the whole concept of what a cocktail could be: no longer a goodly dose of base spirit lightly modified with bitters and sugar or a spoon of liqueur, the cocktail could become something more sleek and urbane. Vermouth soon became the 'bartender's ketchup', finding its way into nearly every new drink recipe that debuted during and after the 1880s.

The current standard recipe for the Manhattan follows a mnemonic based on Manhattan's area code, 212: two ounces bourbon whiskey, one ounce sweet vermouth, two dashes Angostura bitters. Earlier recipes followed the general trend for vermouth in drinks and inverted the ratio of vermouth to whiskey; they are also agnostic about what kind of bitters to use and call for rye instead. This recipe doffs its hat to tradition by using rye, but splits the difference between the historical and the modern by using a 50/50 split of whiskey to vermouth.

INGREDIENTS

45 ml (1½ fl oz) rye whiskey
45 ml (1½ fl oz) sweet red vermouth
1 dash orange bitters
1 dash aromatic bitters
maraschino cherry, to garnish (optional)
orange peel, to garnish (optional)

METHOD

Build ingredients in a mixing glass. Add ice and stir until chilled. Strain into a chilled coupe glass. Garnish with either a maraschino cherry on a skewer or a twist of orange peel.

Depending on who you ask, the Margarita was invented at Rancho la Gloria by Carlos 'Danny' Herrera in 1938, or at Hussong's Cantina by Don Carlos in 1941, or at Tommy's Place by Francisco 'Pancho' Morales in 1942 ... The only Margarita origin story that we can safely disregard is the one about Margaret 'Margarita' Sames inventing the drink for a dinner party in Acapulco in 1948, simply because the American importer of José Cuervo tequila was already using the Margarita to advertise their wares three years earlier.

The truth about the Margarita might be more banal: that nobody really 'invented' it, because it's a simple riff on a pre-Prohibition classic, the Daisy. The Daisy emerged in the 1870s as a sour sans egg white and charged up with a little hit of fizzy water. Before too long, it was being sweetened with dashes of the cordials du jour: things like curaçao, triple sec and yellow Chartreuse. Take the earliest, orange-flavoured iterations of the Daisy and swap the whiskey or brandy out for tequila, and you have something that bears a close resemblance to a contemporary Margarita. But the clincher for this theory is simple: the word *margarita*, in Spanish, means 'daisy'.

The tequila-based Daisy was a Mexican specialty until the 1950s, when it attracted mainstream attention in the United States. By the early 1970s it was a cultural phenomenon – the first frozen Margarita machine was invented in Dallas in 1971 to keep up with demand. Quality tequilas were hard to come by in the 1970s, which may have led to the drink's devolution (blended strawberry Marg, anyone?), but – thanks to the work of agave proselytisers such as tequila expert Julio Bermejo – high-quality, 100 per cent agave tequilas are abundant these days, which means it's the perfect time to rediscover the joys of this most popular – and most maligned – of tequila drinks.

INGREDIENTS

lime wedge, to rim the glass

sea salt, to rim the glass

45 ml (1½ fl oz) tequila

30 ml (1 fl oz) curaçao or triple sec

15 ml (½ fl oz) lime juice

lime wedge or wheel, to garnish

METHOD

Prepare an Old Fashioned or coupe glass by moistening the outside of its rim with a lime wedge and dipping it in sea salt. Leave it to dry, then chill in the freezer.

Build ingredients in a cocktail shaker. Add ice and shake thoroughly to chill. Double-strain into the prepared chilled glass (top with fresh ice if using an Old Fashioned glass). Garnish with a lime wedge or wheel.

he story goes something like this: a gold miner, about to face a long, cold journey from San Francisco to the mining town of Martinez, stops in at the Occidental Hotel for a little something to warm him up. He bellies up to the bar, where he is attended by none other than Jerry Thomas, 'the Jupiter Olympus of the bar' (as Thomas called himself in his 1862 book *Bar-Tender's Guide*). After the miner explains his reason for seeking a comforting drink, he is given an original cocktail, magnanimously named after his destination. Thus the Martinez, the predecessor of the modern-day Martini, is born.

It's a good story, but there's just one problem with it – nobody knows whether or not it's true. It has a few facts going for it: Thomas did indeed tend bar at the Occidental in the 1860s, just after publishing the *Bar-Tender's Guide*, and indeed one of the earliest recipes for the Martinez appears in the 1887 edition of the same book. Unfortunately, by that stage Thomas had been dead for two years, and, in any case, Thomas had a bad track record of taking credit for drinks whose genesis he had nothing to do with – such as the Tom and Jerry, despite evidence that it existed years before his birth. Perhaps it shouldn't surprise anyone that a man who had a set of solid-silver barware custom-made for him, and who also owned two white rats named Tom and Jerry that perched on his shoulders as he mixed drinks, might be liable to tell a tall tale or two. The good burghers of the town of Martinez, for their part, vigorously insist that it, not San Francisco, was the birthplace of the drink.

You can forgive the parties involved for wanting to stake a claim on the drink. With a little bit of fiddling – swap old tom gin for dry; French vermouth for the Italian; orange bitters for the aromatic; axe the maraschino, change the ratios – you can create something that looks an awful lot like the later Dry Martini. And *that* drink went on to become the iconic drink of the post-Prohibition cocktail world … but that, as they say, is another story.

INGREDIENTS

60 ml (2 fl oz) sweet red vermouth
30 ml (1 fl oz) old tom gin
5 ml (¼ fl oz) maraschino liqueur
1 dash aromatic bitters
lemon peel, to garnish

METHOD

Build ingredients in a mixing glass. Add ice and stir until chilled. Strain into a chilled coupe glass. Garnish with a twist of lemon peel.

When the craft cocktail movement started in earnest at the turn of the millennium, a new style of bar began to appear. These bars were more than simply watering holes where you could get a well-crafted drink – they were also ambassadors for a different approach to drink-making and hospitality, and their presence invariably altered the way the local hospitality scene operated. For Brisbane, Australia, that bar was the Bowery – and it was its original Mesha cocktail that made the Bowery a success story.

The Bowery opened in 2003, inspired by the American bars that owner Stephanie Canfell experienced in New York City: a heady mixture of dive bars, local bars and hotel bars such as the Waldorf Astoria and the Plaza. The resulting Brisbane bar was the kind of place you could go to for an immaculately crafted classic cocktail, but also the kind of place that was packed to the gills on Friday and Saturday nights.

The Mesha was commissioned for the Bowery from London-based bartender Barry Chalmers, who was keen to experience a change of scenery by moving to Australia. Chalmers sent the recipe over before arriving in Brisbane, where he found that the drink had become the star of the Bowery's second cocktail list. It's not hard to see why – with its Żubrówka base (see page 161) it appealed to drinkers who had cut their teeth on the vodka craze of the late 1990s, while the pineapple juice and falernum syrup gave the drink a tropical tiki touch that fits perfectly with Brisbane's humid subtropical climate. It also helped that the drink came out an alluring shade of pink (thanks to the raspberry purée) and with a cinnamon sugar rim.

Brisbane's cocktail scene has grown exponentially more sophisticated, but the Mesha was the drink that marked Brisbane as a place that made well-crafted cocktails.

INGREDIENTS

lime wedge, to rim the glass
cinnamon sugar, to rim the glass
40 ml (1¼ fl oz) Żubrówka vodka
20 ml (¾ fl oz) apple liqueur
20 ml (¾ fl oz) pineapple juice
15 ml (½ fl oz) falernum
15 ml (½ fl oz) lime juice
5 ml (¼ fl oz) raspberry purée
(or 3–4 fresh raspberries, muddled)
apple slices, to garnish

METHOD

Prepare a coupe glass by moistening the outside of its rim with a lime wedge and dipping it in cinnamon sugar. Leave it to dry, and then chill in the freezer.

Build ingredients in cocktail shaker. Add ice and shake until chilled. Double-strain into the prepared coupe glass. Garnish with a fan of thin apple slices.

METAMORPHOSIS

KARLOVY VARY, CZECH REPUBLIC

When Gregor Samsa wakes up to find himself transformed in Czech author Franz Kafka's short story 'The Metamorphosis', the question of just *what* Samsa has become is left open-ended. Samsa becomes an *ungeheuren Ungeziefer* (enormous vermin), but English-speaking readers are accustomed to thinking of Samsa as a bug, particularly a giant cockroach. It's therefore apt that this cocktail – named after Kafka's story and featuring the very Czech bitters Becherovka – has a murky, unappealing cockroach-brown hue. Overcome any revulsion you might have towards it, though, because the Metamorphosis is a great showcase for one of the Czech Republic's finest alcoholic products.

Becherovka bitters comes from Karlovy Vary, the Czech spa town formerly known as Carlsbad. Karlovy Vary's 12 hot springs and the mineralised waters that come from them attracted visitors from all over central Europe who sought to cure their ailments. In 1805, German count Maximilian von Plettenberg-Wittem zu Mietingen visited Karlovy Vary with his own personal physician, the English doctor Christian Frobrig, and the pair stayed with local pharmacist Josef Vitus Becher. Frobrig gave Becher a recipe for his own medicinal bitters, which Becher went on to tweak. Commercial pro-duction of Becherovka – first called Becher's Karlsbader Englisch-Bitter – commenced in 1807. It would take Josef's son, Johann, to turn Becherovka into the powerhouse it is today; he built Becherovka's first plant and oversaw its growing popularity with Czech drinkers. It's not hard to see why Czech drinkers took to Becherovka: with its complex bouquet of cinnamon, cloves, ginger and menthol, it remains utterly delicious.

Given that Becherovka goes back to the cocktail's infancy, it's a little perplexing to discover that it does not have an extensive history of use in cocktails. It's mostly enjoyed on its own, or in a simple highball with tonic water (a 'Beton'). But this cocktail by Jackson Cannon of Boston's Eastern Standard bar riffs off the Prohibition-era classic Bee's Knees to create an elegant introduction to Becherovka. *Na zdraví* (cheers)!

INGREDIENTS

45 ml (1½ fl oz) Becherovka bitters
22 ml (¾ fl oz) honey syrup (see tip)
22 ml (¾ fl oz) lemon juice
lemon peel, to garnish

METHOD

Build ingredients in a cocktail shaker. Add ice and shake to chill. Double-strain into a chilled coupe glass. Garnish with a twist of lemon peel.

BARTENDER'S TIP: To make honey syrup, mix equal parts (by volume) of honey and very hot water. Stir until completely dissolved, decant into a sterilised bottle and store in the refrigerator.

MINT JULEP
LOUISVILLE, KENTUCKY

iny Louisville, Kentucky, surely punches above its weight when it comes to cocktails. It is the home of one pre-Prohibition classic – the Pendennis Club – and makes a passionate (if somewhat historically dubious) claim on another, the Old Fashioned. Perversely enough, the cocktail most commonly associated with Louisville is one that wasn't even invented there – the Mint Julep, which was named the official cocktail of the Kentucky Derby in 1938. We owe it to the Derby for keeping the Mint Julep alive and well.

As David Wondrich argues in his book *Imbibe!*, the name 'julep' is a bit of a joke. The word descends from the Persian *gulāb*, and it first entered the English language as a synonym for medicine. American colonists took to calling their morning tots a 'julep' in much the same way some people call Coca-Cola 'the black doctor' for their hangover cure. But by 1793 'julep' had come to refer to a specific kind of drink: a mixture of spirit, water and sugar, enlivened by mint. When the American ice industry expanded in the early 1800s (see page 133), the Mint Julep acquired its *pièce de résistance*: the finely crushed ice that turned it into the very essence of refreshment on a hot day in a state like Kentucky.

The Mint Juleps of this era were a far cry from the Juleps you can now find at the Kentucky Derby. They were more often than not built on brandy rather than bourbon whiskey, and they quite frequently contained all sorts of what we would now see as adulterants, such as splashes of port wine or floats of Jamaican rum. Their garnishes were ornate by our current standards – not just mint, but fresh berries and wheels of lemon, all dusted with a fine coating of powdered sugar. This recipe splits the difference between the 19th-century Julep and the one we know and love.

INGREDIENTS

5–6 mint leaves
15 ml (½ fl oz) simple syrup
60 ml (2 fl oz) bourbon whiskey
15 ml (½ fl oz) dark rum (something strong and pungent)
3 mint sprigs, to garnish
fresh berries, to garnish (optional)
lemon wheels, to garnish (optional)

METHOD

Place mint and simple syrup in a metal julep cup (or Old Fashioned glass). Muddle mint and sugar lightly. Add whiskey and fill cup with finely crushed ice. Stir until a frost forms on the outside of the cup. Top with more crushed ice. Using the back of a bar spoon, float dark rum over the drink. Garnish with 3 sprigs of mint, lightly slapped, and – if you feel like it – fresh berries in season or wheels of lemon.

MOJITO

HAVANA,
CUBA

Englishman Sir Francis Drake was a feared privateer (read: pirate), so it's fitting that a little bit of that fear has rubbed off on the Mojito, the drink he supposedly helped inspire and that bartenders love to hate. The Mojito is a descendant of El Draque (see page 21), a Caribbean potion of cachaça, lime and mint that was supposedly invented in the 16th century to settle Drake's stomach; however, the reason bartenders currently hate it has more to do with the excesses of the late 1990s and early 2000s than with the English pirate who was the scourge of the Spanish Main.

El Draque cocktail was eventually rendered a little less fearsome as El Draquecito, a drink that appears in Ramón De Palma's 1838 novella *El Cólera en La Habana*. De Palma's Draquecito would have been made with *aguardiente de caña*: firewater made from sugarcane. But then came the new, lighter style of rum, Bacardí, which had been filtered for purity and created using a special strain of yeast. Whip yourself up a Draquecito with Bacardí rum, add a splash of sparkling water and serve it on some ice, and you've got something worthy of a new name. In West Africa, a *mojo* is a cloth bag filled with the magician's tools of the trade – why not call it a 'Mojito', or a 'little spell'?

After emerging in the 1910s – apparently first served at a bar called La Concha – the Mojito became Havana's drink of choice, and it has kept that position ever since. As drinks historian Wayne Curtis puts it, 'If you walk into any Old Havana bar ... and hold up two fingers without comment, the odds are favourable you'll get two Mojitos in return.'

Despite Havana's love for the drink, it didn't really catch on in the United States and the rest of the world until the end of the 20th century, when it became the thirst-quencher du jour for the popped-collar fraternity set. That unfortunate association – as well as the time-consuming nature of the drink's preparation – has made it one of the modern bartender's least-favourite concoctions. Spare yourself the hassle of rolled eyes and long waits by making one at home instead.

INGREDIENTS

6–8 mint leaves
22 ml (¾ fl oz) simple syrup
60 ml (2 fl oz) white rum
30 ml (1 fl oz) lime juice
60 ml (2 f l oz) sparkling water
mint sprig, to garnish

METHOD

Lightly muddle mint leaves and sugar syrup in the base of a Collins glass. Add rum and lime juice. Top with finely crushed ice and stir to incorporate. Finish by filling glass with sparkling water and topping with more crushed ice if necessary. Garnish with a sprig of lightly slapped mint. Sip slowly through a straw.

NEGRONI

FLORENCE, ITALY

ount Camillo Negroni was one hell of a dude: a famous gambler, fencing teacher and former rodeo cowboy who, according to legend, strolled into Florence's Caffè Casoni one day in 1919 and asked the bartender, Fosco Scarselli, to replace the soda in his Americano cocktail with something with a little bit more kick, like gin. With that request, the famous Negroni was born. The story's almost too good to be true, which is why so many bartenders and cocktail historians took the larger-than-life Count to be a work of fiction whipped up by Campari's marketing team.

But while many cocktail origin stories turn out to be a flimsy tissue of half-truths, suppositions and guesswork, thanks to some hard legwork by drinks historians David Wondrich and Gary Regan, we know that there really was a Count Camillo Negroni of Florence, who truly did spend time in the United States as a rodeo cowboy, and who did indeed ask Fosco Scarselli for the drink that now bears his name. Notwithstanding some heated controversy about one General Pascal Olivier Count de Negroni, claimed by his descendants to have been the originator of the drink, the case for Count Camillo currently appears to be a slam-dunk.

Despite its attractive origin story, the Negroni is the kind of drink you might kindly call a late bloomer. It first appeared in print under the name Camparinete Cocktail in 1929, and remained relatively neglected outside of its homeland (apart from a cameo appearance in the hands of James Bond) until the craft cocktail boom of the 2000s transformed it, rather suddenly, from a C-list historical curiosity to an A-list classic, right up there with the Martini, the Manhattan and the Old Fashioned.

Some serve up this drink stirred over ice and strained into a chilled coupe glass, and others serve it long, in a tall glass with a good splash of sparkling water. While both of these are delightful, this recipe cleaves to Italian tradition, which serves the Negroni short over ice, and in equal parts.

INGREDIENTS

30 ml (1 fl oz) gin (see tip)
30 ml (1 fl oz) sweet red vermouth
30 ml (1 fl oz) Campari
orange peel, to garnish

METHOD

Build ingredients in a mixing glass. Add ice and stir until well chilled. Strain into an Old Fashioned glass and top with fresh ice. Garnish with a twist of orange peel.

BARTENDER'S TIP: This recipe is best made with a classic London dry gin and an orthodox sweet vermouth – save the fancy stuff for other, better-suited drinks.

NEGRONI SBAGLIATO

MILAN, ITALY

Every good bartender knows the importance of *mise en place* – that is, having everything at hand and in the right place. When the bar gets packed and you're 'in the weeds', you find yourself relying on muscle memory to work at pace with the array of ingredients behind the bar. So if someone puts something in the *wrong* place – say, the prosecco bottle where the gin bottle should be – and you go to make a drink – say, a Negroni (see page 94) – well, the resulting product would be a disaster, right?

Fortunately for us cocktail drinkers, there is such a thing as serendipity. When bartender Mirko Stochetto accidentally grabbed a bottle of prosecco instead of gin while making a Negroni at Bar Basso in Milan one busy night in the early 1970s, what came out was less a disaster and more of a masterpiece. The Negroni Sbagliato – Italian for 'Mistake Negroni' or 'Wrong Negroni' – functions as something of a missing link between various bitter aperitivo cocktails. You could look at it as a lighter, fizzy version of a Negroni, or as a beefier Campari Spritz, with sweet vermouth in place of the sparkling water. However you consider it, this beautiful accident has the virtue of being incredibly easy to make and completely delicious.

More serendipity: the Negroni Sbagliato happened to be born in Milano, home not only to Campari's first production plant, but also to the Milano-Torino cocktail: a simple 50/50 mixture of Campari (Milano) and sweet red vermouth (Torino). The Milano-Torino begat the Americano, which is merely a Milano-Torino charged with sparkling water, and the Americano begat the Negroni, which emerged when the rough-and-tumble Count Camillo Negroni asked for an Americano stiffened with gin in place of the sparkling water. Little wonder, then, that the Negroni Sbagliato has found a place in the firmament of Italian aperitivo beverages. The only mystery that remains is why it took *quite* so long for serendipity to strike …

INGREDIENTS

30 ml (1 fl oz) Campari
30 ml (1 fl oz) sweet red vermouth
90 ml (3 fl oz) prosecco (see tip)
orange wheel, to garnish

METHOD

Build Campari and sweet vermouth in an Old Fashioned glass and top with prosecco. Add ice gently (in order not to dissipate the fizz). Garnish with a wheel of orange.

BARTENDER'S TIP: The strong bitterness of the Campari will dominate the prosecco, so don't feel obliged to use the best one you can afford – go for cheap and cheerful instead.

NINETEEN
TWENTY-FOUR

COLOMBO,
SRI LANKA

If you feel bad about how far the once-mighty Batavia arrack (see page 129) has fallen, spare a thought for Goa arrack. This palm-sap spirit, which was responsible for introducing the British to the joys of punch, is completely unavailable on the world market, despite its importance to the history of drink-making. It is still made in the contemporary state of Goa, India, under the name fenny, but owing to Indian liquor laws can't be sold outside of the state. Its popularity and prestige there has been eclipsed by another distillate, also named fenny (based on the fruit of the cashew tree). It's fortunate, then, that something close to the old Goa arrack can still be found – just made a little further south, in Sri Lanka.

Sri Lankan palm arrack is made from the sap of the coconut palm. This sap is collected by 'toddy tappers', who scale the trees, slice open the flower bud and place a pot underneath the flowing sap. The sap needs to be collected in the cool of dawn, as it will quickly begin to ferment thanks to airborne yeasts and Sri Lanka's hot climate. Once this toddy has been fermented into palm wine, it is distilled and aged in halmilla-wood casks. The resulting spirit is a lighter, more refined product than its brawny cousin Batavia arrack and tastes lightly nutty and malty, with distinct coconut and floral notes.

Unfortunately, much of the arrack made in Sri Lanka is a mass product for the local market and only a little is exported. But growing interest in Batavia arrack and the revival of punches as drinks of interest have meant that high-quality palm arracks from Sri Lanka can now be found on the global market. The Nineteen Twenty-Four cocktail was developed for Rockland Distilleries's Ceylon Arrack brand by bartender Ondřej Pospíchal (and is named after the year Rockland was founded). It demonstrates the versatility of palm arrack by using it as the base spirit for a sophisticated aperitif. Try it – if you're lucky enough to find a bottle.

INGREDIENTS

40 ml (1¼ fl oz) Sri Lankan palm arrack
20 ml (¾ fl oz) manzanilla sherry
15 ml (½ fl oz) maraschino liqueur
10 ml (¼ fl oz) sweet red vermouth
lemon peel, to garnish

METHOD

Build all ingredients in a mixing glass. Add ice and stir until well chilled. Strain into a chilled coupe glass. Garnish with a twist of lemon peel.

BARTENDER'S TIP: Look for an arrack made with 100 per cent coconut palm spirit – cheaper brands are often a mix-ture of palm spirit and neutral alcohol.

OAXACA OLD FASHIONED
OAXACA, MEXICO

hroughout the 20th century, mezcal was one of the most under-appreciated spirits on the planet. Aside from a starring role in Malcolm Lowry's booze-soaked tragedy *Under the Volcano* (see page 157), it was renowned – if it could be called renowned at all – for being cheap dross, a rough spirit that would burn like hellfire on the way down and that came in a bottle with a worm at the bottom. You might have heard the old canard that 'mezcal is to tequila as brandy is to cognac', a claim that implies that mezcal is an inferior version of its more refined and famous sibling. While it's technically true – until recently, tequila was indeed defined as a specific type of mezcal – it's out of date: mezcal now has its own protected denomination of origin and can rival even the finest tequila.

Both mezcal and tequila ultimately come from agave – a genus of succulent plants native to Mexico. The core of these plants (called the *piña*, owing to its resemblance to a pineapple) is roasted and pressed to release its sweet juices, which are then fermented and distilled. This is where the similarities between the two end. For tequila, only one species of agave, the agave azul, can be used, while mezcal can utilise over 30 different species of agave plant. The agave for tequila is roasted in industrial ovens, while the agave for mezcal is usually roasted in wood-fired pit ovens, which lends mezcal its characteristic smokiness. Tequila's production is centred on the state of Jalisco, while mezcal's is centred further south, in Oaxaca.

Mezcal's current popularity in the craft cocktail scene owes much to two importers of the spirit – Ron Cooper, the founder of Del Maguey mezcal, and John Rexler, owner of Guatemala's Café No Sé – as well as bartenders such as Texas's Bobby Heugel and New York's Ivy Mix and Phil Ward. This mezcal twist on the traditional Old Fashioned was invented by Ward in 2007 and has become something of a modern classic since. The original version uses a split base of tequila and mezcal, but this version suggests using a full 60 ml (2 fl oz) of a mellow *añejo* (aged) mezcal.

INGREDIENTS

60 ml (2 fl oz) añejo mezcal
5 ml (¼ fl oz) agave nectar
2 dashes chocolate mole bitters
orange peel, to garnish

METHOD

Build ingredients in a mixing glass. Add ice and stir to chill. Strain into an Old Fashioned glass and top with fresh ice. Garnish with a twist of orange peel.

BARTENDER'S TIP: If you can't acquire a mellow añejo mezcal, you can create a split base by using 45 ml (1½ fl oz) high-quality (100 per cent agave) reposado tequila and 15 ml (½ fl oz) pungently smoky *joven* (unaged) mezcal.

PAINKILLER
JOST VAN DYKE,
BRITISH VIRGIN ISLANDS

The Soggy Dollar Bar, on the island of Jost Van Dyke in the British Virgin Islands, is about as paradisiacal as a beach bar can get: pure white sand blazing in the sunlight, a ragged fringe of palm trees for shade and crystal-clear water in an almost cartoonish shade of aqua. Just one problem: there's no jetty on which to moor your boat, so if you want to grab a drink, you're going to have to swim to shore – ergo the name Soggy Dollar Bar. The bar is renowned for the Painkiller, one of the most-loved cocktails of the modern tropical tiki drink renaissance. Essentially a Piña Colada (see page 106) made with a dark, funky rum and an extra splash of orange juice, the Painkiller is famous not for its origin story, but for a recent unsavoury legal battle.

Invented either by George and Mary Myrick or Daphne Henderson of the Soggy Dollar Bar in 1971, the Painkiller originally called for a mixture of different rums. It couldn't call for Pusser's rum as the now-classic recipe does because, until 1980, no such thing existed – the company got started when entrepreneur Charles Tobias purchased the rights to the blending information used by the British Admiralty to make the rum ration formerly given out to its sailors. This British Virgin Islands–based company later sought the Soggy Dollar Bar's permission to trademark the Painkiller name in the 1990s.

The Painkiller cocktail leapt to prominence in 2011, when Pusser's rum mounted legal action against a New York City tiki bar named Painkiller, who, in response, agreed to change their name to PKNY. This move sparked a debate about the appropriateness of trade-marking cocktails that still persists today.

This recipe cleaves to the original ratio of non-alcoholic ingredients (four parts pine-apple, one part coconut, one part orange), and updates the rum ratio to equal the pine-apple – a tweak suggested by tiki guru Matt 'RumDood' Robold. If you can't find Pusser's rum, make it with any other fragrant dark rum in the English tradition, such as a Jamaican rum – just don't call it a Painkiller ...

INGREDIENTS

60 ml (2 fl oz) Pusser's British
  Navy Rum
60 ml (2 fl oz) pineapple juice
15 ml (½ fl oz) orange juice
15 ml (½ fl oz) coconut cream
  (unsweetened)
7 ml (¼ fl oz) simple syrup
grated nutmeg, to garnish
orange wheel, to garnish
mint sprig, to garnish

METHOD

Build ingredients in a cocktail shaker. Add ice and shake thoroughly to chill. Strain into a tiki vessel of your choice and top with crushed ice. Garnish with freshly grated nutmeg, a wheel of orange and a sprig of lightly slapped mint.

PEGU CLUB

YANGON, MYANMAR

A great deal of cocktail history is tied to colonialism; in fact, it's fair to say that without colonialism, there would be no such thing as the cocktail. Nineteenth-century cocktails relied on exotic ingredients brought from far-flung places, and the less their drinkers knew about the squalid, and often downright exploitative, conditions that prevailed in those locales, the better. And if you were a member of the colonial elite and you felt like enjoying a cocktail, well, you would want to do so in an exclusive environment, away from the hoi polloi you had spent the day exploiting. If you were a British member of Burma's colonial elite, the place you'd take that cocktail was the Pegu Club.

The Pegu Club has a few claims to fame. A young Rudyard Kipling spent his one night in Rangoon (now Yangon) at the club, where the war stories he heard would inspire his poem 'Mandalay'. The club makes a cameo appearance in George Orwell's acidly satirical novel *Burmese Days*, when one of the white *pukka sahibs* (European gentlemen) of Orwell's fictional Kyauktada complains that even the Pegu Club has started admitting 'natives'. But chief among its claims to fame is that the original cocktail made there – a blend of gin, curaçao, bitters and lime juice – has lived on, even though the club building itself has been seized by the Myanmarese government and has slid into dereliction. Harry Craddock's 1930 *Savoy Cocktail Book* calls it a cocktail 'that has travelled, and is asked for, around the world'.

The cocktail's current fame is now owed to bartender Audrey Saunders, an inveterate champion of gin as a spirit, whose Pegu Club bar in New York City remains one of the iconic establishments of the craft cocktail movement. 'In all frankness, it [the Pegu Club cocktail] resurfaced because I rolled up my sleeves and championed it', Saunders told writer Phil McCausland. Despite the unsavoury aspects of its history, this cocktail – a classic lesson in how the whole can transcend its parts – remains a drink worth championing.

INGREDIENTS

60 ml (2 fl oz) gin
22 ml (¾ fl oz) curaçao or triple sec
15 ml (½ fl oz) lime juice
1 dash aromatic bitters
1 dash orange bitters
lime peel, to garnish

METHOD

Build ingredients in a cocktail shaker. Add ice and shake to chill. Double-strain into a chilled coupe glass. Garnish with a twist of lime peel.

PIÑA COLADA

SAN JUAN, PUERTO RICO

L ike the origins of many other drinks in this book, the Piña Colada's are contested. The real argument comes down to a fight between two bars in San Juan that both claim the drink's invention – and even have the plaques to prove it. Barrachina claims that it was invented there by Ramon Portas Mingot in 1963; the Beachcomber Bar at the Caribe Hilton goes one better and offers two conflicting claims of authorship (either Ramón 'Monchito' Marrero Pérez in 1952 or Ricardo García in 1954).

But this most Puerto Rican of cocktails might well have come from elsewhere. A tantalising mention in the *New York Times* on 16 April 1950 (prior to its supposed invention at the Beachcomber Bar) claims that the drink is Cuban, and specifies its ingredients as 'rum, pineapple and coconut milk'. A letter to the editor of the same publication in 1989 claims that the letter-writer was serving Piña Colada cocktails to friends in Mexico in 1950, 'and didn't think there was anything new about them'. But drinks called 'Piña Coladas' would have been all over the Caribbean in the first half of the 20th century – in Spanish, the phrase means 'strained pineapple' and simply referrs to pineapple juice that has been strained free of pulp.

Puerto Rico *can* lay claim to the technology that made the Piña Colada a sensation: a method of extracting coconut cream. Acquiring coconut cream used to be a laborious process – you'd have to extract the coconut's meat, soak it in water, squeeze out the liquid, then wait for the cream to rise. Now, of course, you go to the supermarket and buy a can – made possible by Puerto Rican professor Ramón López Irizarry, who introduced the first brand of coconut cream, Coco López, to the market.

So if you like Piña Coladas (and getting caught in the rain …) break out the blender and raise a glass to Irizarry for taking this little-known Caribbean drink to the world stage.

INGREDIENTS

60 ml (2 fl oz) rum
60 ml (2 fl oz) coconut cream
   (unsweetened)
30 ml (1 fl oz) pineapple juice
22 ml (¾ fl oz) simple syrup
15 ml (½ fl oz) lime juice
pineapple, cherry, orange wheel and/or
   mint, to garnish (optional)

METHOD

Combine the rum, coconut cream, pineapple and lime juices, and simple syrup in a blender. Top with a roughly equal quantity of crushed ice. Blend to combine, starting at the blender's lowest speed and slowly speeding up. Once the blender is at top speed, slowly add more crushed ice until the drink starts to smoothly fold in on itself. Serve in a tiki mug or Collins glass. Garnish liberally with whatever garnishes please you.

It's hard to imagine that the origin of a fairly marginal spirit such as pisco could cause such tension – but then again, nationalism is one hell of a drug, especially when the nation you've been duking it out with was also once your combatant in a brutal war. Both Chile and Peru lay claim to pisco, a clear, lightly aged grape brandy, and the fact that both countries were formerly part of the same territory (the Viceroyalty of Peru) at the time of pisco's invention means that the historical record is hopelessly unclear. The question of the true home of pisco ignites such passion in these two bordering countries that Peruvian pisco, by law, must be labelled as generic *aguardiente* (firewater) in Chile – and vice versa.

The origin of the Pisco Sour is fortunately much clearer. Thanks to the work of Peruvian writer Raúl Rivera Escobar, it can be traced back to Peru in 1903, where it appears in a pamphlet as a recipe simply called 'cocktail'. But it would take an American by the name of Victor 'Gringo' Morris, owner of the American Bar in Lima, to make the world sit up and pay attention to the Pisco Sour. By 1924 Morris was advertising his bar's wares to English-speaking expats in Peru and Chile by claiming that his bar 'has been noted for many years for its "Pisco Sours"'. From the American Bar the Pisco Sour went on to win over the drinking cultures of both Peru and Chile. Regional differences still persist, though – the Chilean version omits the egg white and the decorative drops of bitters on top.

Which kind of pisco you use in the cocktail is up for debate, too: the Chilean style, made in column stills and sometimes lightly aged in wood, is a suave spirit, while the Peruvian style, made in pot stills and rested only briefly in ceramic vessels, is more rustic and flavoursome. While this recipe will work with a Chilean pisco, a robustly-flavoured Peruvian pisco is not only more historically accurate, but will better cut through the silky texture of the egg whites, giving you an excellent Pisco Sour.

INGREDIENTS

60 ml (2 fl oz) pisco (preferably
  Peruvian)
15 ml (½ fl oz) lime juice
15 ml (½ fl oz) simple syrup
1 egg white
3 or 4 drops aromatic bitters
  (preferably Amargo Chuncho)

METHOD

Build all ingredients except the bitters in a cocktail shaker. Dry shake to fluff up, then add ice and shake until chilled. Double-strain into a chilled coupe glass. Drop bitters onto the foamy surface of the drink and gently run a toothpick through the drops to create a swirling pattern.

PLANTER'S PUNCH
KINGSTON, JAMAICA

The Planter's Punch is the template from which all subsequent tropical tiki drinks derive. When legendary American bartender Ernest Gantt – better known by his later nom de booze, Don the Beachcomber (see page 79) – first encountered it on the Patio Bar of the Myrtle Bank hotel in Kingston in the 1920s, it was love at first sight. After the repeal of Prohibition, and thanks to the work of popularisers like Gantt, Planter's Punch became the drink du jour in America. As tiki historian Jeff 'Beachbum' Berry argues, it also became the template for all of Gantt's tiki drinks, which were themselves the template for the almighty Mai Tai (see page 78).

For years a bit of Caribbean doggerel circulated about how to make a Planter's Punch: 'This recipe I give to thee, / Dear brother in the heat. / Take two of sour (lime let it be) / To one and a half of sweet [sugar]. / Of Old Jamaica [dark rum] pour three strong, / And add four parts of weak [water]. / Then mix and drink. I do no wrong – / I know whereof I speak.' Planter's Punch is, therefore, little more than a glass of plain rum punch prepared à la minute, with whatever fancy additions (sparkling water, grenadine, pineapple juice) the maker feels like contributing.

By the 1920s nearly every bar and hotel in the Caribbean could whip up something approximating a Planter's Punch, but Kingston was known as the cradle of the drink thanks to Fred L. Myers. As the owner of Jamaican rum brand Myers's Rum, Myers had flipped the old 'one of sour, two of sweet, three of strong, four of weak' to the less poetic but more potent 'one of sweet, two of sour, three of weak, four of strong'. This version follows Myers's improved proportions, and it incorporates a 1957 suggestion from American Colonel A.R. Woolley, managing director of the Lemon Hart rum company: cold black tea instead of water for the 'weak'.

INGREDIENTS

60 ml (2 fl oz) dark Jamaican rum
45 ml (1½ fl oz) freshly brewed black tea, chilled
30 ml (1 fl oz) lime juice
22 ml (¾ fl oz) simple syrup
cherry, to garnish (optional)
lime wheel, to garnish (optional)
mint sprig, to garnish (optional)

METHOD

Build ingredients in a Collins glass. Top with finely crushed ice and swizzle with a wooden swizzle stick or bar spoon. Top with more crushed ice. Garnish as you wish with a lime wheel, cherry and/ or mint sprig.

BARTENDER'S TIP: Don't brew the tea too strongly – aim for the strength of a regular cup of black tea.

PRUSSIAN GRANDEUR PUNCH

BERLIN, GERMANY

There was a lot of Prussian grandeur going about in the late 19th century. Thanks to a series of wars, cannily manoeuvred by Prussian chancellor Otto von Bismarck, the fractious German-speaking states (with the notable exception of Austria) were unified into the German Empire in 1871. Prussia was clearly the dominant state: it was the largest, and the newly crowned Kaiser Wilhelm I came from there. While Kaiser Wilhelm theoretically ruled the new German Empire from Berlin, it was his chancellor, Bismarck, who truly controlled the country. Bismarck would have put Machiavelli to shame and was a powerful conservative authoritarian – the 'iron chancellor'.

The creator of the Prussian Grandeur Punch, Harry Johnson, knew a thing or two about Prussia. Born in the former Prussian capital of Königsberg (now Kaliningrad, Russia) in 1845, he emigrated with his family to San Francisco at the age of seven. By 1860, at the tender age of 15 (or so he claimed), he was mixing drinks at the Union Hotel. Johnson claimed to have beaten Jerry Thomas (see page 85) to the authorial punch by writing the first-ever bartender's manual around this time, but none of the 10,000 copies supposedly printed have yet shown up. Later, in 1882, he published a 'new and improved' (or perhaps first) edition of this *Bartender's Manual*, which appeared as a bilingual edition in both English and German.

The Prussian Grandeur Punch in the 1882 *Bartender's Manual* certainly packs a strong one-two. It features six whole bottles of *branntwein* (a German vodka-like spirit made from rye, now better known as korn), as well as a bottle each of caraway-flavoured *kümmel* and cherry-based *kirschwasser*. And the Prussian connection? Well, the brand of branntwein called for by Johnson, Nordhäuser, happened to be Bismarck's favourite. This recipe scales the drink down from Johnson's Herculean proportions to a quantity suitable for home use.

INGREDIENTS

115 g (4 oz) raw sugar
330 ml (11 fl oz) filtered water
750 ml (25 fl oz) korn
125 ml (4 fl oz) kümmel
125 ml (4 fl oz) kirschwasser
20 ml (¾ fl oz) anisette
20 ml (¾ fl oz) curaçao
lemon and orange wheels, to garnish

METHOD

Combine sugar and water in a large punchbowl and stir until dissolved. Add all other ingredients and stir thoroughly to incorporate. Chill in the refrigerator. Before serving, place a large block of solid ice in the punchbowl to keep the contents cool. Garnish with wheels of lemon and orange.

SERVES 10

PUNCH À LA ROMAINE
SOUTHAMPTON, ENGLAND

When the famed RMS *Titanic* left Southampton on its maiden voyage to New York City in 1912, the Punch à la Romaine (or Roman Punch) had reached the height of its fame, having been popularised by French chef extraordinaire Auguste Escoffier. Punch à la Romaine would have its final, morbid claim to fame aboard the *Titanic*. Menus recovered from the ship name this cocktail as the sixth course – a palate-cleanser between rich dishes – in the first-class banquet dinner on the night the so-called 'unsinkable' ship hit an iceberg and sank into the Atlantic's freezing waters. For the hifalutin elites aboard, this end to the party must have come as a rather rude shock.

The *Titanic*'s tragic demise would be followed by more terrible world events – the assassination of Austrian archduke Franz Ferdinand, which led to World War I; not long after that war's conclusion, the Volstead Act in America would usher in Prohibition. Punch à la Romaine's labour-intensive preparation and expensive ingredients – in true Edwardian style, the original called only for the best French champagne – ensured it would not be at home in this new world, and its fortunes essentially sank alongside the *Titanic*.

But if you want to party like it's your last night on Earth, or simply wish to cleanse your palate between courses of lamb and squab, you could do worse than whipping up a few glasses of Punch à la Romaine, which manages the feat of being both silkily opulent (courtesy of the egg white) and refreshing (thanks to the acidity of the lemon and sparkling wine). More advanced versions of the recipe require an ice-cream maker to churn a lemon granita, as well as an Italian meringue prepared in advance – but this streamlined version uses crushed ice to replicate the granita's texture and makes the meringue in the shaker.

INGREDIENTS

30 ml (1 fl oz) flavourful white rum
   or blanc rhum agricole
30 ml (1 fl oz) orange juice
15 ml (½ fl oz) lemon juice
15 ml (½ fl oz) simple syrup
1 egg white
60 ml (2 fl oz) sparkling wine
orange zest or peel, to garnish

METHOD

Build all ingredients except sparkling wine in a cocktail shaker. Dry shake to fluff up, then add ice and shake until chilled. Strain into a large coupe glass; add finely crushed ice until the mixture resembles a granita. Top with sparkling wine. Garnish with fresh orange zest or thin ribbons of orange peel.

While not exactly a cocktail mecca, the Philippines has had an outsized impact on the history of mixed drinks. Without the galleon trade route between Manila and Acapulco, Mexico, tequila as we know it might not have existed: some archaeologists believe Filipinos were the first to introduce distillation to Mexico. And while the figureheads of the tropical tiki drink movement were white Americans, much of the hard work done in tiki bars during the 1930s and 1940s was carried out by Filipino bartenders labouring in literal obscurity.

The cocktail first came to the Philippines in wartime. In order to prevent an attack on the United States's west coast in the Spanish–American War of 1898, American ships sailed into Manila's harbour and destroyed the Spanish fleet stationed there. The Philippine independence movement, helmed by Emilio Aguinaldo, initially welcomed American involvement as an opportunity to achieve liberation from the country's Spanish colonists – but quickly realised that the United States wished to assume control over the Philippine archipelago. By 1899 the independence movement had declared war on the US, which swiftly retaliated, violently repressing the Filipino movement.

The Philippines officially became a territory of the United States, and military force was dispatched to keep it that way – and where Americans went, a thirst for cocktails swiftly followed. Thus, when the American writer and drink-lover Charles H. Baker arrived in the American-controlled Philippines in 1926, he witnessed how the cocktail had adapted to local conditions.

Baker was so impressed by the local cocktail scene that he listed 17 Filipino cocktail creations in his 1939 book *The Gentleman's Companion*. Many of his recipes came from Walter Ellett 'Monk' Antrim, the manager of the Manila Hotel, including this mixological oddity, which Baker claims as the 'number one favourite in Manila, where it even outstrips the perennial Dry Martini'.

INGREDIENTS

45 ml (1½ fl oz) white rum

7 ml (¼ fl oz) gin

7 ml (¼ fl oz) dry vermouth

7 ml (¼ fl oz) lemon juice

7 ml (¼ fl oz) orange juice

7 ml (¼ fl oz) simple syrup

5 ml (¼ fl oz) dry anis or 2 dashes absinthe

1 egg white

lemon peel, to garnish

METHOD

Build all ingredients in a cocktail shaker. Dry shake to fluff up, then add ice and shake until chilled. Double-strain into a chilled coupe glass. Garnish with a twist of lemon peel.

QUEEN'S PARK SWIZZLE

PORT OF SPAIN, TRINIDAD AND TOBAGO

Angostura bitters got its start in 1824 when German Dr Johann Siegert was looking for a cure-all medicine, while working as the surgeon-general for Venezuelan military leader Simón Bolívar and living in the Venezuelan town of Angostura (now Ciudad Bolívar). Before long Siegert's bitters had become the key ingredient in the quintessential drink of the British naval officer, Pink Gin, and from there wound its way into liquor cabinets and back bars the world over. After Venezuela's political climate destabilised, Siegert's sons moved the company to Port of Spain, Trinidad and Tobago, where Angostura bitters has been produced ever since.

Unlike its many competitors, Angostura survived the devastation of Prohibition, and the distinctive bottle with its oversize label – apparently the result of a miscommunication between the person responsible for ordering the bottles and the person who designed the label – soon became something of a staple for bartenders throughout the 20th century. No bar worth the name would be found without a bottle of Angostura, even if it hadn't been touched for years.

In recent years the craft cocktail boom has brought forth a panoply of new bitters, from restorations of Angostura's former competitors (such as Abbott's bitters) to a dizzying array of wild new concoctions (grapefruit oolong bitters, anyone?). While Angostura might now seem old hat, the Queen's Park Swizzle – named after the now-demolished Queen's Park hotel in central Port of Spain, a short jaunt from Angostura's headquarters – will remind you exactly why this delightfully balanced bitters stuck around when its peers were dropping like flies. With its rich, rosy crown of bitters floating on top and a hefty pour of rum inside, it's little wonder that tiki drink pioneer Trader Vic called it 'the most delightful form of anaesthesia given out today'.

INGREDIENTS

8 mint leaves
60 ml (2 fl oz) flavourful dark rum
20 ml (¾ fl oz) lime juice
5 ml (½ fl oz) simple syrup
6–8 dashes Angostura bitters
mint sprig, to garnish

METHOD

Lightly muddle mint leaves in the base of a Collins glass. Add rum, lime juice and simple syrup and stir to incorporate. Top with finely crushed ice and swizzle with a wooden swizzle stick or bar spoon. Top with more crushed ice. Crown with dashes of Angostura bitters. Garnish with a sprig of lightly slapped mint and sip slowly through a straw.

BARTENDER'S TIP: Take care when dashing large quantities of Angostura bitters – they will permanently stain almost anything they come into contact with.

RHUBARB FIZZ

SYDNEY, AUSTRALIA

U ntil recently, Sydney's bar scene was dominated by nightclubs and other large venues with steep fees, door lists and velvet ropes to keep the hoi polloi out. Loads of glitz and glam, of course, as suits Australia's most fashion-conscious city, but the drinks were … not necessarily memorable. All of that changed with the introduction of small bar licenses to Sydney's CBD in 2007, which allowed smaller operators a chance to open without having to bear the prohibitive licensing costs imposed on the bigger players. A veritable boom of small bars ensued – chief among them Bulletin Place, a tiny attic venue that serves a rotating list of cocktails based on what local produce that is fresh and in season.

Bulletin Place's focus on freshness ties in with a broader shift in Australian eating and drinking habits. Movements such as 'loca-vorism' and 'slow food' – which emphasise eating locally sourced and organic food – have developed alongside a growing recognition of the environmental and social impacts of globalisation. Australian bartenders have started to look closer to home rather than opting for prestigious imported products. Perhaps it is appropriate, then, that Bulletin Place has none of the high-gloss polish of Sydney's ritzier venues, instead opting for a small space with exposed beams and deco-rated with reclaimed furniture.

A tangy blend of fresh Australian rhubarb compote and gin, sweetened with Pedro Ximénez sherry and balanced with lemon juice, the Rhubarb Fizz is a deceptively simple drink that reveals a serious amount of thought on the part of its inventor, Bulletin Place co-owner Tim Philips. And, fortunately, if you live anywhere that rhubarb can grow, you can re-create it in your home bar without compromising its local and seasonal ethos.

INGREDIENTS

40 ml (1¼ fl oz) gin
20 ml (¾ fl oz) rhubarb compote (see tip)
15 ml (½ fl oz) lemon juice
10 ml (¼ fl oz) Pedro Ximénez sherry
10 ml (¼ fl oz) simple syrup
1 egg white
60 ml (2 fl oz) sparkling water

METHOD

Combine all ingredients except sparking water in a cocktail shaker. Dry shake to fluff up, then add ice and shake until chilled. Add sparkling water to a Collins glass and slowly double-strain shaker's contents over it. Add fresh ice, if desired.

BARTENDER'S TIP: You can find many recipes online for homemade rhubarb compote. You only need three ingredients to make it: rhubarb, sugar and water.

SAKURA MARTINI

KOBE, JAPAN

While cocktail culture may have been introduced to Japan relatively early (see page 7), cocktails made with distinctly Japanese ingredients remained a rarity on the global cocktail scene until the late 20th century. And when these drinks did appear – including the iconic Australian Japanese Slipper (see page 68) – they hardly epitomised the Japanese approach to craft cocktails. Perhaps those grouped under the 'Saketini' umbrella are the worst offenders: flavoured by a few tokenistic 'Asian' ingredients, such as lychee or cucumber, and often overbearingly sweet.

Part of the problem is that Western cocktail makers have stubbornly seen 'sake' as a single, unchanging ingredient rather than the breathtakingly diverse and changeable product it is. Sake is rice wine, made from rice that has been polished (in order to remove the bran) then mixed with water and fermented. And the Nada area in and around Kobe is regarded as the epicentre of Japan's sake industry. Like wine, sake is divided into a dizzying array of different categories: daiginjō-shu (made from rice that has had half its weight polished away), junmai (without added distilled alcohol) and tokubetsu honjōzō-shu ('special' brew, with added alcohol) to name a few. These categories can be further divided depending on how the sake's fermentation is started and how it is treated after fermentation concludes. A cocktail recipe that just calls for 'sake' is a bit like a cocktail recipe that just calls for 'wine' without specifying whether that wine is red, white, fortified or sparkling – a recipe so vague as to be useless.

Japanese bartender Kenta Goto's Bar Goto features distinctively Japanese riffs on classic cocktails, each composed with the attention to detail and fastidiousness that has made the Japanese approach to craft cocktails famous. Bar Goto's Sakura Martini – with its salted cherry blossom floating delicately in the coupe glass, and with quality sake playing the starring role – showcases both Japanese ingredients and a Japanese sensibility to the craft cocktail world.

INGREDIENTS

1 salted sakura (cherry) blossom, to garnish
75 ml (2½ fl oz) junmai taruzake sake (preferably Ozeki Komatsu Tatewaki)
30 ml (1 fl oz) gin (preferably Plymouth)
1 dash maraschino liqueur

METHOD

Rehydrate salted sakura blossom in a small bowl with hot tap water for 10 minutes. Strain using a sieve and rinse with cold water. Drain and gently pat dry with paper towel. Set blossom aside. Build sake, gin and maraschino in a mixing glass. Add ice and stir until well chilled. Strain into a chilled coupe glass. Garnish with the sakura blossom.

SAN MARTÍN

MONTEVIDEO, URUGUAY

The cocktail first made its way to South America thanks to travelling *yanquis* (Americans) of the late 19th and early 20th centuries, who took a taste for mixed drinks with them wherever they went. When these Americans arrived in Uruguay and Argentina, they encountered European immigrants (drawn by opportunities in the lucrative livestock business), who had brought with them their taste for the old world's complex, herbaceous potables – things like absinthe, vermouth and various amari (digestives). Trade along the Río de la Plata and the Río Paraná would make Uruguay's capital, Montevideo (as well as the Argentine cities of Rosario and Buenos Aires), a thriving, modern metropolis. It was in this melting pot of the Platine basin that the premier classic cocktail of South America, the San Martín, was forged.

As cocktail historian David Wondrich notes, the San Martín is merely a sweet Martini with a South American accent. And the name? José Francisco de San Martín was one of the foremost *libertadores* (freedom fighters) of South America. Wondrich contends that 'when the loud hosannas for the Martini that American drinkers were emitting finally echoed down to the tip of that long and fascinating continent the name [was] heard somewhat differently, "Martini" becoming "Martín", and if you've got a Martín a 'San' must surely be lurking in the vicinity'.

Early sources agree that the San Martín consists of equal portions of gin (London dry or old tom) and sweet vermouth enlivened with a splash or two of ... well, here's where it gets tricky. It seems nearly every bar in the Platine basin made the San Martín in a different way – dashed with some combination of orange bitters, maraschino liqueur, cherry brandy, curaçao or yellow Chartreuse. The earliest-known recipe, from 1911, calls for three separate additives to the gin and vermouth template, but this recipe, from influential Belgian bartender Robert Vermeire's *Cocktails: How to Mix Them*, simply adds a bar spoon of yellow Chartreuse, adding more than enough herbaceous complexity to make this San Martín, making it more than a mere Martini clone.

INGREDIENTS

45 ml (1½ fl oz) gin or old tom gin
45 ml (1½ fl oz) sweet red vermouth
5 ml (¼ fl oz) yellow Chartreuse
lemon peel, to garnish
fresh fruit, to garnish (optional)

METHOD

Build ingredients in a mixing glass. Add ice and stir until chilled. Strain into a chilled coupe glass. Garnish with a twist of lemon peel and, optionally, fresh fruits in season.

SAZERAC

NEW ORLEANS, USA

The Sazerac, the official cocktail of New Orleans, took many years to be established as a separate drink from the Whiskey Cocktail (which itself eventually came to be called the Old Fashioned (see page 18). The Sazerac traces its lineage back to the 1830s, when New Orleans–based apothecary Antoine Amedie Peychaud developed the proprietary bitters that now bear his name. These bitters were whipped up into a cocktail alongside some sugar, water and a hefty dose of French brandy – preferably cognac from the Sazerac de Forge et Fils company, which would eventually lend this drink its name. By 1843 you could find many New Orleans bars adding a dash of absinthe, and something approaching the modern Sazerac was born.

But two twists of fate awaited the drink that would come to be called the Sazerac: phylloxera and the absinthe panic. The phylloxera louse, an American grape parasite that was introduced to Europe in the middle of the 19th century, devastated Europe's wine industry, and therefore its brandy industry. With French brandy a rarity, New Orleans bartenders started making cocktails with American rye whiskey instead. The rarity of French wine and brandy also partly led to the increased popularity of absinthe in France. Known for its high alcohol content and the potentially hallucinogenic properties created by the inclusion of wormwood (hence its nickname *la fée verte*, or the green fairy), absinthe consumption soon led to a moral panic. Thus many recipes for the Sazerac call for Herbsaint (a wormwood-free absinthe substitute) rather than absinthe itself.

The Sazerac's name first appeared in print in 1899 – prior to when absinthe bans kicked in – and early recipes didn't always call specifically for Peychaud's bitters. Rather than aiming for an illusory authenticity, this version of the Sazerac uses a split base of cognac and rye whiskey, plus some absinthe and an extra dash of Angostura bitters, to reflect this noble drink's chequered history.

INGREDIENTS

30 ml (1 fl oz) cognac

30 ml (1 fl oz) rye whiskey

7 ml (¼ fl oz) simple syrup

2 dashes Peychaud's bitters

1 dash aromatic bitters (optional)

5 ml (¼ fl oz) absinthe (or Herbsaint)

1 twist of lemon peel

METHOD

Build all ingredients except absinthe in a mixing glass. Rinse a chilled Old Fashioned glass with the absinthe, coating all the surfaces, and discard the excess. Add ice to the mixing glass and stir cocktail until chilled. Strain cocktail into absinthe-rinsed glass. Express the oils from a twist of lemon peel over the surface of the drink and either discard the twist or rest it on the rim of the glass.

SEVEN SEAS SWIZZLE

JAKARTA, INDONESIA

Before there was rum, there was Batavia arrack. This funky, rough-and-ready Indonesian spirit – distilled from sugarcane molasses that has been fermented with cakes of dried and mouldy red rice and a splash of palm wine – is still made in much the same way in Indonesia as it has been for centuries. Though it might seem unusual to the modern palate, it was, alongside its cousin Goa arrack (see page 99), largely responsible for introducing the West to the joys of distilled spirits.

Despite what we now think of as its characteristic roughness, Batavia arrack used to be prized for its suavity compared to other spirits. While the lower classes were getting sloshed on gin (see page 55), 'rack punch' was the drink of choice for England's dissolute upper classes of the 18th century. But by the start of the 19th century a taste for arrack punch was seen as quaint or to be regarded with amusement – it appears in iconic bartender Jerry Thomas's 1862 *Bar-Tender's Guide* as a curio: 'but little used in America, except to flavor punch'. Its survival into the 21st century has much to do with the Dutch, who acquired a taste for it while colonising Indonesia, and also due to the invention of Swedish Punsch, a Batavia arrack–based liqueur still popular in Sweden today (see page 34).

Just as other antique spirits have been resurrected, so too has Batavia arrack, which now appears in craft cocktail bars across the world. It is highly unlikely to supplant either rum or brandy in popularity again, but it does have a cult following among bartenders, including New York City bar Porchlight's Nick Bennett, whose Seven Seas Swizzle – a mashup of the Queen's Park Swizzle (see page 118) and a traditional tea-based punch – showcases the spirit's unusual virtues.

INGREDIENTS

60 ml (2 fl oz) Batavia arrack

22 ml (¾ fl oz) green tea syrup (see tip)

15 ml (½ fl oz) lime juice

1 dash orange bitters

mint sprig, to garnish

grated nutmeg, to garnish

METHOD

Build ingredients in a Collins glass. Top with crushed ice and swizzle with a wooden swizzle stick or bar spoon. Top with more crushed ice. Garnish with a sprig of lightly slapped mint and freshly grated nutmeg. Sip slowly through a straw.

BARTENDER'S TIP: To make green tea syrup, mix equal quantities of sugar and very strong, freshly-brewed green tea. Stir until sugar is dissolved, let cool, transfer to a sterilised bottle and store in refrigerator.

SHANGHAI BUCK
SHANGHAI, CHINA

t's 1941 in New York and John G. Martin, an executive at spirit company Hueblein Inc., sits down at the bar at the Chatham Hotel. He's had an awful day. Ever since the day in 1939 that he convinced Hueblein to buy the US rights to a little brand called Smirnoff, he's barely been able to sell the stuff. Sure, he made inroads with the promise that 'Smirnoff leaves you breathless', but that only made his new acquisition look even less respectable. Jack Morgan, owner of Hollywood bar Cock 'n' Bull, commiserates; he's had a heck of a time trying to shift the spicy ginger beer he brewed especially for his bar. A travelling salesperson joins in; he can't get people to fork out for the copper mugs he's been trying to sell. Someone has the bright idea of combining Martin's strange Russian spirit, some ginger beer and a squeeze of lime, and serving it in one of the copper mugs. Voilà – the Moscow Mule is (supposedly) born.

When those three travellers joined forces to make the Moscow Mule, they were working from an older template, the Buck – a combination of spirit, ginger ale or beer, and citrus. Vodka isn't the only spirit you can make a Buck from: make it with American whiskey and you have a Whiskey Buck; make it with Scotch and you have a Mamie Taylor; or make it with white rum and you have a Shanghai Buck. But why call it a Shanghai Buck when white rum originates in Cuba? As travelling *bon vivant* Charles H. Baker notes in his 1939 book *The Gentleman's Companion*, Shanghai 'consumes – or did consume, at least, before the Japanese issue – more Bacardí rum than any other city on Earth'.

While its similarity to the Moscow Mule may have rendered the Shanghai Buck something of a footnote in the annals of cocktail history, its difference from the Moscow Mule may ultimately bring it back into the repertoire of the contemporary drinker. White rums are no longer solely the province of the Bacardí family – whose flagship Carta Blanca product has erred on the side of smoothness over complexity since its forced exile from Cuba in 1960 – and bold, complex white rums can now be found in back bars all over the world. Perhaps now is the time for the Shanghai Buck to make a comeback.

INGREDIENTS

60 ml (2 fl oz) white rum

15 ml (½ fl oz) lime juice

120 ml (4 fl oz) ginger beer

lime wedge or wheel, to garnish

METHOD

Build white rum and lime juice in a Collins glass, and top with ginger beer. Add ice and garnish with a wedge or wheel of lime.

SHERRY COBBLER

JEREZ, SPAIN

As strange as this may seem to contemporary drinkers, there was a time when ice was a complete luxury and therefore absent from cocktails. But Bostonian entrepreneur Frederic Tudor was determined to bring ice to the masses – and he did so a century before the invention of the refrigerator and freezer.

In 1805, Tudor planned to ship naturally forming ice from New England's lakes and ponds to the tropics. His plan was met with derision and a flat refusal from established shippers to take on ice as cargo – an obstacle he surmounted by simply buying a ship of his own. Alas, when his clipper arrived in Martinique in the Caribbean, the ice mostly intact, there was nowhere to store it. Tudor watched his hopes of making a profit literally melt away. Decades later – after the establishment of a series of icehouses around the world, and thanks to inventor Nathaniel Wyeth's horse-drawn ice-cutter – the concept of buying ice took off, making Tudor an incredibly wealthy man.

Perhaps not surprisingly, ice was soon used to cool the heels of the booze du jour, sherry, a fortified wine made in and around Jerez, Spain. By 1838 the Sherry Cobbler had come to be a good measure of sherry poured over 'cobbles' of crushed ice, livened only with a spoonful of sugar and a garnish of fresh fruit. In 1843 it had its first celebrity endorsement, courtesy of Charles Dickens, who encountered the drink during his American tour and featured it in the novel *Martin Chuzzlewit*. Its cameo in the novel gives us insight into early 19th century drinking – and the importance of straws. As drinks historian David Wondrich argues in his book *Imbibe!*, 'the state of 19th-century dentistry dictated that if at all possible [ice] be kept away from direct contact with people's teeth'. Poor Martin, the protagonist of Dickens's tale, has never seen a drinking straw before and is flabbergasted by the suggestion that he place it in his mouth. Fortunately, he eventually does: 'Martin took the glass, with an astonished look; applied his lips to the reed; and cast up his eyes once in ecstasy'. After you try a Sherry Cobbler, you'll understand Martin's reaction.

INGREDIENTS

90 ml (3 fl oz) fino, manzanilla, amontillado, palo cortado or oloroso sherry

15 ml (½ fl oz) simple syrup

orange wheel, to garnish

seasonal fruit (optional)

METHOD

Build ingredients in a cocktail shaker. Add ice and shake thoroughly to chill. Strain into an Old Fashioned glass or Collins glass. Top with crushed ice. Garnish with wheels of orange or other fruits in season. Serve with a straw.

ognac, the king of brandies, owes its invention to a few historical accidents. Dutch traders began shipping salt, paper and wine from the Charente region of southern France in the late 16th century, bound for England, the Netherlands and Scandinavia. The fragile white wines of the time didn't travel well, so the Dutch traders ran them through stills to create *brantwijn* (burnt wine), now better known as brandy. Soon enough the Charentais people figured out that double distillation provided high-quality brantwijn, resting the spirit in oak casks improved it, and certain kinds of grapes better suited distillation. The area around the town of Cognac became renowned worldwide for its brandies – even if the French themselves now much prefer cognac's more rustic cousin, armagnac.

Possibly the most famous cognac cocktail there is, the Sidecar possesses a number of competing origin stories. David A. Embury, in his 1948 book *The Fine Art of Mixing Drinks*, claims that the Sidecar 'was invented by a friend of mine at a bar in Paris during World War I and was named after the motorcycle sidecar in which the good captain was customarily driven to and from the little bistro where the drink was born and christened'. But then why is the recipe in the 1923 edition of Harry MacElhone's *ABC of Mixing Cocktails* credited to Patrick MacGarry, head bartender of London's Buck's Club? And what exactly does Robert Vermeire mean when he says in his 1922 *Cocktails: How to Mix Them* that it is both 'popular in France' and 'introduced in London by MacGarry'?

And just what is the recipe? Everyone agrees on the ingredients – cognac, triple sec or curaçao and lemon juice – but the proportions are all over the map, reflecting the difficulty of balancing the drink's three basic elements. More than most cocktails, the Sidecar demands careful calibration – use this recipe as a template, and explore from there.

INGREDIENTS

sugar, to rim the glass (optional)

45 ml (1½ fl oz) cognac

22 ml (¾ fl oz) curaçao or triple sec

22 ml (¾ fl oz) lemon juice

orange peel, to garnish

METHOD

Build ingredients in a cocktail shaker. Add ice and shake thoroughly to chill. Double-strain into a chilled coupe glass (add your sugar rim first, if you're having one). Garnish with a twist of orange peel.

BARTENDER'S TIP: New York bartender Joaquín Simó 'fattens' his Sidecars with 5 ml (¼ fl oz) of rich demerara sugar syrup (two parts sugar to one part water). Try it if you feel your Sidecar is a little lenten.

SINGAPORE SLING

SINGAPORE

sk any bartender about the invention of the Singapore Sling and they'll answer something like this: Ngiam Tong Boon, 1915, at the Long Bar of the Raffles Hotel. Ask them what's *in* one – well, that's another story. Gin, obviously (the drink is a direct descendent of the plain Gin Sling). And something to make it pink (cherry liqueur, grenadine, dashes of Angostura bitters or even a red wine float). The rest seems to be up for debate.

Thanks to the Singapore National Library's digitised archives, as well as some hard work by cocktail historian David Wondrich, we have a much better picture of the origins of this famous drink. Singapore's British colonisers certainly seemed to enjoy a Gin Sling or two, with mentions of the drink popping up in the 1890s. By 1903, 'pink slings for pale people' were being served at a going-away party for Australian racing personality 'Daddy' Abrams. A decade later, in 1913, a controversy would roil in the Singaporean papers about whether the Singapore Cricket Club would deign to serve something so vulgar as a Gin Sling. The *Weekly Sun* reported an ingenious workaround from two club members, who ordered 'one Cherry Brandy, one Domb [i.e. D.O.M. Bénédictine], one Gin, one Lime Juice, some Ice and water, a few dashes of Bitters – and then enjoyed a really decent Sling'.

What then of Ngiam Tong Boon, the Raffles Hotel and the pineapple juice in the 'official' version? Whether invented there or not, the Sling was very much associated with the Raffles: Charles H. Baker encountered the Sling there in 1926, and wrote rapturously about it. When Raffles was renovated and reopened as a luxury hotel in the 1970s, pineapple juice–based tropical drinks were all the rage. The recipe from the Raffles leans very heavily on the pineapple juice now and incorporates triple sec, but the version presented here is based on the 1913 workaround by those thirsty Singapore Cricket Club members and is much less ornate.

INGREDIENTS

45 ml (1½ fl oz) gin
30 ml (1 fl oz) lime juice
22 ml (¾ fl oz) cherry brandy
22 ml (¾ fl oz) Bénédictine
2 dashes aromatic bitters
60 ml (2 fl oz) sparkling water
lime peel, to garnish
brandied cherry, to garnish

METHOD

Build all ingredients except sparkling water in a cocktail shaker. Add ice and shake thoroughly to chill. Double-strain into a Collins glass. Top with sparkling water and add fresh ice to fill. Garnish with a twist of lime peel and a brandied cherry on a skewer.

SOVIET CHAMPAGNE PUNCH

MOSCOW, RUSSIA

The Russian revolution that saw Tsar Nicholas II executed (see page 23) radically changed Russia's orientation towards the rest of the world. The capital moved back east, from Europeanised St Petersburg to its former home in the very Russian city of Moscow. There was now a clash of ideologies: Russian communism versus Western capitalism. Communism promised a world free from material deprivation and want, and by 1935, it appeared to have come good on that promise. Thanks to Joseph Stalin's ruthless policies of industrialisation (and his quiet extermination of his opponents), a brand-new metro system had opened in Moscow, work had begun on the gargantuan Palace of the Soviets, and the shelves of Moscow's food stores groaned under the weight of luxury foodstuffs. To wash it all down, there was champagne – the former drink of class enemies and capitalists, now available in mass quantities and for a reasonable price.

The 'champagne' that first landed in Moscow grocery stores in 1934 wasn't, of course, the real deal from capitalist France. It was instead *Sovetskoye shampanskoye* (Soviet champagne), a curious invention by Anton Frolov-Bagreyev. A chemist by training, Frolov-Bagreyev had taken part in the failed revolution of 1905 and had been exiled to Siberia, but after the successful revolutions of 1917 he was made head oenologist at state-run winery Abrau-Dyurso. By 1934 he had invented a method to perform secondary fermentation (which gives champagne its fizz) in large tanks rather than in the bottle (as it is traditionally done). With manual labour lessened, and ageing sped up with added oak chips, the Soviet government could create huge quantities of champagne-like wine quickly and cheaply.

Though the USSR is no more, Sovetskoye shampanskoye lives on in former Soviet countries, where it remains a popular tipple, despite some objections to both the 'Sovetskoye' and 'shampanskoye' halves of the name. But you don't need Sovetskoye shampanskoye to enjoy this punch – any dry sparkling wine will do.

INGREDIENTS

300 ml (10 fl oz) dry sparkling wine, chilled

300 ml (10 fl oz) dry white wine, chilled

150 ml (5 fl oz) sweet white muscat wine, chilled

75 ml (2½ fl oz) Bénédictine

75 ml (2½ fl oz) cognac or other brandy

tinned fruit, to garnish

METHOD

Mix ingredients in a medium punchbowl. Add a large block of solid ice to keep contents cool. Garnish bowl and individual cups with tinned fruit.

SERVES 6

The Spritz Veneziano – a fizzy, wine-based drink that appears lurid red or orange – seems like the least butch drink in the world, but it comes with a surprisingly military backstory. After Napoleon's first defeat and exile to Elba in 1814, Europe's powers met in Paris and re-drew the continent's borders; as part of this treaty, the Austrian royal house of Habsburg-Lorraine asserted their claim over the Venetian Republic, and sent in their military to make sure the locals knew who was running the show.

Enter the spritzer. Venetian lore has it that the occupying soldiers found the local white wines too robust by comparison to the rieslings and grüner veltliners that they were accustomed to. Their ingenious solution was to add a *spritz* (spray) of water to soften the blow. When the soda syphon became commonplace towards the end of the 19th century (long after the Austrians had relinquished their claim), that splash of water was often carbonated. But the real innovation came in the 1920s, when Venetian bartenders started to add Italy's own aperitivo bitters to the mixture.

Exactly what kind of aperitivo bitters was first included remains contentious, but there is no doubt about which brand of aperitivo bitters dominates the Spritz as we know it today: Aperol, a brand born in Padova, not far from Venice, in 1919. A Spritz made with Aperol is bubbly, faintly bittersweet and decidedly moreish. Other versions of the Spritz take on the character of their aperitivo: the Campari Spritz is robustly bitter, the Cynar Spritz is smoky and brooding, and the Select Spritz is light and elegant. Two last refinements in the 1990s give us the Spritz Veneziano we know today – the use of a sparkling Prosecco rather than still wine for extra fizz, and the addition of ice to keep things cool during long summer days of drinking on the beach of Venice's Lido di Jesolo. *Cin cin* (cheers)!

INGREDIENTS

60 ml (2 fl oz) aperitivo bitter of your choice (such as Aperol, Select, or Campari)

90 ml (3 fl oz) prosecco or other dry sparkling wine, chilled

30 ml (1 fl oz) sparkling water

orange wedge, to garnish

green olives, to garnish

METHOD

Build ingredients in an Old Fashioned or wine glass. Add ice gently. Garnish with a wedge of orange, and green olives on a skewer.

BARTENDER'S TIP: If you are feeling particularly brave or retro, replace the prosecco with a Venetian pinot grigio or a richer, rounder soave.

The history of Prohibition is an object lesson in unintended consequences. In the United States, the Volstead Act made an exception for alcohol made for medicinal purposes – a loophole that eventually caused paralysis in those who drank medicinal Jamaica Ginger that bootleggers had adulterated with a neurotoxin to make it taste better.

Iceland's national spirit, Brennivín (a potato-based, caraway-flavoured spirit), has a friendly nickname that stems from Prohibition. In an attempt to discourage the consumption of spirits after the repeal of Prohibition in 1935, the state-owned spirits monopoly labelled Brennivín with a black label bearing a picture of a white skull, which led Icelanders to start calling it *svarti dauði*, or 'black death'. This nickname, combined with the strikingly minimalist black label on the green bottle, and its general unavailability outside of Iceland, has given Brennivín something of a cult status in the wider world, even though Icelanders themselves tend to be ambivalent about the stuff. Both filmmaker Quentin Tarantino and musician Dave Grohl are fans: Budd drinks Brennivín from the bottle in Tarantino's *Kill Bill: Vol. 2*, and Brennivín makes a cameo appearance in the lyrics to the Foo Fighters's song 'Skin and Bones'. And now, thanks to that cult status, Brennivín is finally available in a few places outside of Iceland.

The Stone Crush, by New York–based bartender Chaim Dauermann, descends from a post-shift shot of Brennivín (then hand-imported and illegal to sell over the bar) chased with Steigl beer. One of Dauermann's colleagues at the Up and Up bar Instagrammed the drink and added the hashtag #Brennivín – which caught the attention of Brennivín's US importer, who was finalising arrangements to bring it into the country. Now that Brennivín is legal to sell, the Up and Up offers a fancified version of the post-shift drink, enlivened with vermouth and rhubarb-flavoured amaro.

INGREDIENTS

3 or 4 wheels of cucumber
45 ml (1½ fl oz) Brennivín
15 ml (½ fl oz) white sweet vermouth
(blanc/bianco vermouth)
7 ml (¼ fl oz) Rabarbaro Zucca
30 ml (1 fl oz) pilsner
1 lemon peel
cucumber wheels, to garnish

METHOD

Muddle cucumber in a cocktail shaker, then add all other ingredients except pilsner. Add ice and shake thoroughly to chill. Double-strain into an Old Fashioned glass and add pilsner, then top with fresh ice. Express the oils from a twist of lemon peel over the drink, then discard the twist. Garnish with fresh wheels of cucumber.

SUFFERING BASTARD

CAIRO, EGYPT

I t's one thing to invent a hangover pick-me-up, and quite another to do so with limited resources in a war zone. For that act alone Joe Scialom, bartender at Shepheard's Hotel in Cairo, Egypt, deserves our praise. That his hangover cure may well have helped defeat Erwin Rommel's Nazi troops – well, that's quite the cherry on the cake.

Conditions in Cairo towards the end of 1942 (in the middle of World War II) can't have been pretty: Germany's feared general Rommel was inching towards the city, looking to cut off Allied supply lines. Good booze was scarce, and the British troops holding him off at nearby El Alamein were in need of a drink when on leave. In this grim atmosphere, Scialom – an Italian Jew who had wound up tending bar in Cairo – came to work one day in desperate need of a hangover cure. His creation, which included bitters compounded at a pharmacy across the street, not only worked its magic on Scialom itself, but proved to be something of a hit among the British troops. The Suffering Bastard was born.

According to tiki drink historian Jeff 'Beachbum' Berry, the Suffering Bastard also played a small role in the battle of El Alamein – the decisive battle that turned the tides against Nazi Germany's incursion into North Africa. At the height of the battle, Scialom received a telegram from xthe frontlines: 'Can you please send 8 gallons [30 litres] of Suffering Bastard, everyone is really hung-over'. Scialom frantically filled every container he could find with the concoction and dispatched it to El Alamein in taxis, perhaps worried that without it, Rommel's boast that he would soon be drinking champagne at Shepheard's might well come true. Fortunately for both Scialom and us, it didn't.

This recipe cleaves closely to the original – although the spirits you'll use will no doubt be nicer than those available in Cairo in 1942.

INGREDIENTS

30 ml (1 fl oz) gin

30 ml (1 fl oz) brandy or bourbon whiskey

15 ml (½ fl oz) lime juice cordial

2 dashes aromatic bitters

120 ml (4 fl oz) ginger beer, chilled

orange wheel, to garnish

mint sprig, to garnish

METHOD

Build all ingredients except ginger beer in a cocktail shaker. Add ice and shake until chilled. Double-strain into an Old Fashioned or Collins glass. Top with ginger beer and add fresh ice. Garnish with an orange wheel and a mint sprig.

When French king Louis XV offered tokaji aszú (now commonly known as tokay) to his mistress, Madame (or Marquise) de Pompadour, he declared it *'vinum regum, rex vinorum'* – the wine of kings and the king of wines. Louis might have been gilding the lily in an attempt to charm the petticoats off the Marquise, but it's fair to say that tokaji aszú is one of the world's foremost fine wines. The Tokaj region of Hungary was the first wine area where individual vineyards were classified by quality, and it was also the site of the first wines to be made with botrytised grapes, with their increased sugar concentration. Tokaji aszú was the preferred tipple of not only the French court but also of Peter the Great, Emperor Franz Josef and many popes (who, apparently, sipped the rarest and most expensive type of tokaji aszú, called eszencia, on their deathbeds).

The secret to tokaji aszú's concentrated flavour is *Botrytis cinerea*, a mould that grows naturally on the skin of the region's grapes. As it grows and searches for water, it punctures the skin of the grapes and slowly dehydrates them, which concentrates the juice's sugar and acid content. These 'azsú' grapes are individually handpicked and pressed into a paste, while the non-botrytised grapes are made into a base wine. The aszú paste is then blended with the base wine. The more aszú that goes in, the more sweet, voluptuous and – unfortunately – expensive the resulting wine is going to be.

Tokaji was unfortunately hit hard by phylloxera (see page 127), then by both world wars, then by communist rule, before making a remarkable comeback in the 1990s. Some reasonably priced examples are now available on the global market, ready to be shaken up into a cocktail – such as this one, a tokaji-infused variation on the classic Smash format, invented by bartender Liam Davy for London steak restaurant and cocktail bar Hawksmoor's Seven Dials location.

INGREDIENTS

1 wedge lemon
2 chunks fresh pineapple
70 ml (2¼ fl oz) tokaji azsú or late-harvest tokaji
15 ml (½ fl oz) apricot liqueur
15 ml (½ fl oz) lemon juice
pineapple wedge, to garnish
mint sprig, to garnish

METHOD

Muddle pineapple and lemon in the bottom of a cocktail shaker. Add remaining ingredients. Add ice, seal shaker and shake thoroughly until chilled. Double-strain into a Collins glass. Top with crushed ice. Garnish with a pineapple wedge and a sprig of mint.

TORONTO
TORONTO, CANADA

The American tax lawyer and amateur mixologist David A. Embury was full of opinions, and he had no reservations about sharing them in his book *The Fine Art of Mixing Drinks*, one of the wittiest and most acerbic books about drinking that has been set to print. On Canadian whisky, he said: 'Just a quick word about Canadian whisky (which, in my opinion, is all it deserves) ... I don't like it.'

Despite Embury's aversion to it, a few of the drinks in *The Fine Art of Mixing Drinks* call for Canadian whisky; of these, the Toronto cocktail is most interesting. In Embury's book, it is essentially an Old Fashioned made with a bar spoon or two of Fernet-Branca, 'a bitters particularly well-loved of Italians'. A nice drink, to be sure, but what on Earth does it have to do with the Canadian city? Given that the Toronto first appears in print in *The Fine Art of Mixing Drinks*, the question remained unresolved until Canadian bartenders Shawn Soole and Solomon Siegel found a recipe in Robert Vermeire's 1922 *Cocktails: How to Mix Them* titled 'Fernet Cocktail'. Basically an Old Fashioned made with either cognac or rye ('to taste') and Fernet-Branca, the cocktail is appended with a brief note: 'This cocktail is much appreciated by the Canadians of Toronto.'

This Fernet Cocktail is undoubtedly the predecessor of the Toronto – but why the switch from cognac or rye to Canadian whisky? Prohibition killed the American whiskey industry by halting distillation for nearly 14 years. When Prohibition was repealed in 1933, there was little American whiskey to go around, but Canadian distilleries were chomping at the bit to get their product back into the United States. Faced with a choice between rough young American whiskeys and smooth, cheaply produced blended Canadian whiskys, American consumers opted for the Canadian option, which dominated the American marketplace. The Canadian whisky industry has changed profoundly since then, and now produces a number of high-quality 100 per cent rye whiskies such as Alberta Premium. Reach for one of these when you mix up a Toronto.

INGREDIENTS

60 ml (2 fl oz) high-quality
   Canadian whisky
7 ml (¼ fl oz) Fernet-Branca
7 ml (¼ fl oz) simple syrup
orange peel, to garnish

METHOD

Build ingredients in a mixing glass. Add ice and stir to chill. Strain into a chilled coupe glass. Garnish with a twist of orange peel.

BARTENDER'S TIP: Look for a 100 per cent rye Canadian whisky: Alberta Premium is a good choice if you can find it.

TRIDENT

TRONDHEIM, NORWAY

f you're worried about the carbon footprint of the bottles in your liquor cabinet, you'd better steer clear of globetrotting linjeakevitt. This Norwegian specialty was accidentally invented in 1805, when, the brig *Trondhjems Prøve* set sail from Trondheim, Norway, for Batavia (now Jakarta, Indonesia), carrying stockfish, hams, cheeses and five casks of Norwegian aquavit – a caraway-flavoured Scandinavian spirit closely related to gin. The food sold quickly to the hungry Dutch colonialists of Batavia, but the aquavit remained untouched: why buy expensive imported spirits when good arrack (see page 129) was being made right there in Batavia?

When *Trondhjems Prøve* returned to Norway in December 1807, the barrels of aquavit were opened and tasted, and the tasters noted that the extremes of heat and cold had profoundly altered the spirit inside – and for the better. Soon aquavit companies were deliberately sending their spirits on voyages to Australia and back in second-hand sherry casks, and linjeakevitt – from *linje*, the equatorial line – was born.

The Trident cocktail, from Seattle-based cocktail proselytiser Robert Hess, is a riff on the classic Negroni (see page 94). Hess started by swapping the gin for a Norwegian linjeakevitt, and then decided to make further substitutions along the same lines: the more obscure, artichoke-based Italian amaro Cynar instead of Campari, and oxidatively aged sherry instead of vermouth. A few dashes of peach bitters bind the drink's unusual and disparate flavours together. The resulting cocktail, named after the fact that Norway, Spain and Italy are all historically seafaring countries, went on to become part of the small canon of modern cocktail classics.

INGREDIENTS

30 ml (1 fl oz) linjeakevitt (such as Lysholm Linie) (see tip)
30 ml (1 fl oz) amontillado, palo cortado, or oloroso sherry
30 ml (1 fl oz) Cynar
2 dashes peach bitters
lemon peel, to garnish

METHOD

Build ingredients in a mixing glass. Add ice and stir to chill. Strain into a chilled coupe glass. Garnish with a twist of lemon peel.

BARTENDER'S TIP: Only two brands of linjeakevitt are currently made: Løiten Linie and Lysholm Linie. The latter is much more widely available outside of Norway.

L atvia may well be the most Baltic of the Baltic states. While Estonia remains chummy with its northern neighbour across the gulf of Finland, and Lithuania continues its close and complex ties with Poland, Latvia mostly looks to itself for cultural influence. One place it does *not* look towards for cultural cues is Russia – the country that invaded all three Baltic states in the aftermath of World War II and occupied them until 1991. Yet, somewhat perversely, the story of Latvia's most popular tipple, Riga Black Balsam, begins with the Russian empress Catherine the Great.

In 1752, a mysterious chemist named Abraham Kunze, new to Riga (now the capital of Latvia, but then part of the Russian Empire), developed an elixir of 17 botanicals steeped in liquor, which he sold as a medicine in distinctive clay bottles. According to Latvian lore, Kunze's elixir achieved its first major success when it was used to treat a stomach illness that Catherine the Great had come down with while passing through Riga. Kunze's balsam soon became the therapeutic drink of choice for Latvians. Commercial production of Riga Black Balsam, based on Kunze's original recipe, commenced in 1843 – and it continues to this day, despite a short interruption in the aftermath of World War II.

Riga Black Balsam is now something of a Latvian drinking icon, and is traditionally taken with coffee or blackcurrant juice. With 45 per cent alcohol by volume and a powerful bitterness from its herbs, it elicits strong reactions from tourists and outsiders. The Turkish Delight, from Bar XIII in Riga, smooths out Riga Black Balsam's famously spiky edges with creamy chocolate sesame halva and turns it into a dessert tipple.

INGREDIENTS

30 ml (1 fl oz) Riga Black Balsam (see tip)
75 g (2½ oz) chocolate-flavoured sesame halva
50 ml (1¾ fl oz) gold rum
40 ml (1¼ fl oz) water
30 ml (1 fl oz) simple syrup
3 dashes chocolate mole bitters
grated dark chocolate, to garnish
gold leaf, to garnish (optional)

METHOD

Build all ingredients except garnishes in a blender and blend until the halva is fully incorporated into the liquids. Place halva mixture in a cocktail shaker, add ice, and shake thoroughly to chill. Double-strain into an Old Fashioned glass. Top with fresh ice. Garnish with grated dark chocolate and, if you have it, a square of edible gold leaf.

BARTENDER'S TIP: The Riga Black Balsam is this recipe's lynchpin – accept no substitutes.

TWENTIETH CENTURY

CHICAGO, USA

Train travel is not a particularly glamorous affair these days. But in the early 20th century, when air travel was the preserve of the very wealthy, business passengers relied on trains to travel between cities, and there was a lot of competition for their custom. Few train services were as glamorous as the Twentieth Century Limited, which ran between New York City and Chicago, Illinois. Perhaps that's why it ended up lending its name to British bartender C.A. Tuck's concoction – an intriguing blend of gin, lemon juice, aperitif wine and chocolate-flavoured crème de cacao – decades after the inaugural service left New York's Grand Central Station in 1902.

The Twentieth Century train was renowned for the class and opulence with which passengers were greeted – the idioms 'red carpet treatment' and 'rolling out the red carpet' come from the Twentieth Century's use of red carpets at stations to guide its passengers aboard. Once on board, passengers could avail themselves of services such as a barber, a maid, a valet and even a stenographer on the 20-hour journey. After a significant upgrade in 1938 – when the trip time reduced to 16 hours thanks to the new Hudson locomotive design – the train became something of a party spot. After the dinner service, the dining car would be transformed into a makeshift nightclub named Cafe Century.

The Twentieth Century cocktail didn't fare quite so well in the popular imagination as the train itself. It was largely forgotten until recently, but, thanks to Ted 'Dr Cocktail' Haigh's book *Vintage Spirits and Forgotten Cocktails*, it is now considered one of the key cocktails of the craft cocktail revival. There is a small controversy over whether or not to use the original Lillet blanc in the cocktail; some argue that the formula for Lillet blanc has changed significantly since the 1930s, and that other quinquina wines taste closer to the original Kina Lillet. The Lillet company deny that they've changed the formula – but they would say that, wouldn't they?

INGREDIENTS

45 ml (1½ fl oz) gin
22 ml (¾ fl oz) Lillet or other white quinquina
22 ml (¾ fl oz) lemon juice
15 ml (½ fl oz) white crème de cacao
lemon peel, to garnish

METHOD

Build ingredients in a cocktail shaker. Add ice and shake thoroughly to chill. Double-strain into a chilled coupe glass. Garnish with a twist of lemon peel.

UNDER THE VOLCANO
CUERNAVACA,
MEXICO

B ritish writer Malcolm Lowry's 1947 novel *Under the Volcano* may well be the bleakest book about the effects of alcohol ever written. Its plot is relatively simple: Geoffrey Firmin, a British Consul in the Mexican town of Quauhnahuac (a thinly disguised fictional version of the real Cuernavaca), drinks himself quite literally to death over the course of the *Día de Muertos* (Day of the Dead festival) of 1938. His ex-wife, Yvonne, and half-brother, Hugh, accompany him through a series of booze-soaked misadventures until, having lost Yvonne and Hugh, he starts an argument with local police in a bar. They push him outside, shoot him, and throw his body into a ravine.

Like many other writers and thinkers, Lowry – as a lifelong alcoholic himself – conceived of alcohol as a *pharmakon*: the remedy that is also a poison. In *Under the Volcano*, he sees this insight through to the macabre end. When Yvonne returns to Quauhnahuac early in the morning of the Día de Muertos, she discovers the Consul at his favourite bar taking a drink, he claims, only to calm his delirium tremens. 'It's really the shakes that make this kind of life insupportable', he says. 'But they will stop: I was only drinking enough so they would. Just the necessary, the therapeutic drink.' Alcohol has caused the changes in the Consul's brain chemistry that give him the shakes; yet alcohol is the only thing that brings relief from the tremors. Lowry develops this insight into the dual nature of alcohol to its tragic conclusion. In *Under the Volcano*, the solution that alcohol offers is a final one.

Given the prominence of agave spirits in the narrative of *Under the Volcano* – the Consul puts away a large quantity of tequila, and knows the end is coming when he starts drinking mezcal – there are a number of different modern cocktails that take their name and inspiration from Lowry's book. This one, by Boston bartender Katie Emmerson, matches smoky mezcal (see page 101) with sherry and Italian amaro for a complex, lightly bitter sipping drink.

INGREDIENTS

30 ml (1 fl oz) mezcal (preferably Del Maguey Chichicapa)

30 ml (1 fl oz) cream sherry (preferably Lustau East India Solera)

30 ml (1 fl oz) Amaro Nonino

1 dash chocolate mole bitters

1 orange peel

METHOD

Build ingredients in a mixing glass. Add ice and stir to chill. Strain into a chilled Old Fashioned glass. Flame an orange peel (see page 45) over the top of the drink, but do not garnish.

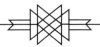

WARD EIGHT

BOSTON, USA

'Never write if you can speak; never speak if you can nod; never nod if you can wink.' So goes the wisdom of 19th-century gangster Martin Michael 'Mohatma' Lomasney, one of the canniest operators in Boston's gritty political history. Lomasney learned the art of realpolitik as a gang leader and bootblack, before befriending a local ward boss and landing work as a lamplighter and health inspector – a job that resulted in an assassination attempt against him in 1894. According to the legend of the Ward Eight's invention, Lomasney was such a consummate politician that he celebrated his election to the Massachusetts General Court in 1898 at the swank Locke-Ober Cafe with a bespoke cocktail named after the ward that delivered the election to him – the night before the election was actually held.

It's a nice story, but Boston historian Stephanie Schorow believes that 'there are holes the size of the old Boston Garden in the generally accepted story of the Ward Eight'. Grenadine was barely seen in the 19th century, but all the rage in the early 20th century, when the oldest-known print reference to the drink emerges. Lomasney and his candidates suffered defeat in that 1898 election season – and Lomasney was a teetotaller and a Prohibitionist, so hardly likely to celebrate any election win with a fancy new mixed drink.

Whatever its origin, the Ward Eight enjoyed a wide following in the 1930s, after the repeal of Prohibition. *Esquire* writer Frank Shay named it one of the ten best cocktails of 1934. In the same year, G. Selmer Fouger, author of the *New York Sun*'s 'Along the Wine Trail' column, asked his readers for information about this hot new drink, and received over 400 replies. One letter contained an interesting twist on the drink: a splash of palo cortado sherry, which serves to add a hint of nutty complexity. This version of the drink is the recipe served at Yvonne's, the supper club that now sits in the former Locke-Ober Cafe space, and was developed with the assistance of drinks historian David Wondrich.

INGREDIENTS

45 ml (1½ fl oz) rye whiskey
15 ml (½ fl oz) palo cortado sherry
15 ml (½ fl oz) lemon juice
15 ml (½ fl oz) grenadine
7 ml (¼ fl oz) orange juice
45 ml (1½ fl oz) sparkling water

METHOD

Build all ingredients except sparkling water in a cocktail shaker. Add ice and shake to chill. Strain into an Old Fashioned glass or goblet, add fresh ice and top with sparkling water.

ŻUBRÓWKA

BIAŁYSTOK, POLAND

While Poland and Russia continue to squabble over who invented vodka, there's no doubt where Żubrówka comes from. This flavoured vodka – infused with the aroma of *Hierochloe odorata*, or bison grass, and made in Białystok, near the Belarusian border – is as Polish as *pierogi* (Polish dumplings). It was first produced in 1928, inspired by the centuries-old Polish aristocratic practice of infusing vodka with bison grass. The bison grass is harvested by hand from glades in the Białowieża forest, lightly dried and infused into vodka, and then a single blade of grass is left in each bottle. The resulting product tastes not only of freshly mown grass, but also of some more ethereal, hard-to-grasp flavours: hints of vanilla, almond, jasmine and tonka bean.

Żubrówka was something of a sensation in bartending circles in the early 2000s – it was vodka, yes, but a vodka that had flavour and character, and could stand up for itself in a cocktail. A simple mixture of Żubrówka and cloudy apple juice (known in Poland as a *szarlotka*, after the Polish for 'apple charlotte') became a cult drink in UK and Australian cocktail culture. But its bewitching aroma spelled trouble in the United States. Part of what makes Żubrówka (and tonka beans) smell so intriguing is the organic compound coumarin – a chemical linked, in high concentrations, to liver problems in rats, and one that is molecularly very similar to the blood thinner Coumadin. The US Food and Drug Administration banned foodstuffs containing any amount of coumarin in 1954, rendering the original Żubrówka illegal. A coumarin-free version named Żu is now available in the US. Somerset Maugham, in his 1944 novel *The Razor's Edge*, makes the original seem worth trying, saying it 'smells of freshly mown hay and spring flowers, of thyme and lavender, and it's soft on the palate and so comfortable, it's like listening to music by moonlight'.

While Żubrówka and apple remains a winning flavour combination, this self-titled cocktail recipe by S.T. Yakimovitch – from W.J. Tarling's 1937 *Cafe Royal Cocktail Book* – showcases the spirit's versatility, producing a delicately spiced aperitif cocktail.

INGREDIENTS

45 ml (1½ fl oz) Żubrówka vodka
45 ml (1½ fl oz) sweet red vermouth
5 ml (¼ fl oz) Danziger goldwasser
1 dash aromatic bitters
1 dash absinthe (optional)
lemon peel, to garnish

METHOD

Build ingredients in a mixing glass. Add ice and stir to chill. Strain into a chilled coupe glass. Garnish with a twist of lemon peel.

INDEX

FURTHER READING

Too many resources were consulted in the writing of this book to be able to name them all. Certain key resources, however, proved invaluable to its development – and I'd recommend that anyone curious about the finer details of this book's cocktails begin their own investigations by picking up the following works.

Print

Arnold, Dave. *Liquid Intelligence: the Art and Science of the Perfect Cocktail.* New York and London: W. W. Norton & Company, 2014

Baiocchi, Talia and Pariseau, Leslie. *Spritz: Italy's Most Iconic Aperitivo Cocktail, with Recipes.* Berkeley: Ten Speed Press, 2016

Baker, Charles H. *The Gentleman's Companion volume two: Being an Exotic Drinking Book, or Around the World With Beaker, Jigger, and Flask.* New York: Crown Publishers, 1946

Berry, Jeff. *Beachbum Berry's Potions of the Caribbean: 500 Years of Tropical Drinks and the People Behind Them.* New York: Cocktail Kingdom, 2013

Brown, Jared and Miller, Anistatia. *Spirituous Journey: a History of Drink* (books one and two). London: Mixellany, 2009-2010

Brown, Jared; Miller, Anistatia; Broom, Dave and Strangeway, Nick. *Cuba: The Legend of Rum.* London: Mixellany, 2009

Craddock, Harry. *The Savoy Cocktail Book.* London: Constable & Company, 1930

Curtis, Wayne. *And a Bottle of Rum: A History of the New World in Ten Cocktails.* New York: Crown Publishers, 2006

Embury, David A. *The Fine Art of Mixing Drinks.* New York: Doubleday, 1948

Haigh, Ted. *Vintage Spirits and Forgotten Cocktails* (revised and expanded ed.). Beverly, Mass.: Quarry Books, 2009

Johnson, Harry. *Bartender's Manual, or How to Mix Drinks of the Present Style.* New York: I. Goldmann, 1888

MacElhone, Harry. *Harry of Ciro's ABC of Mixing Cocktails.* London: Christopher & Company, 1923

MacNeil, Karen. *The Wine Bible* (revised second ed.). New York: Workman Publishing, 2015

Morgenthaler, Jeffrey. *The Bar Book: Elements of Cocktail Technique.* San Francisco: Chronicle Books, 2014

Parsons, Brad Thomas. *Bitters: A Spirited History of a Classic Cure-All.* Berkeley: Ten Speed Press, 2011

Simonson, Robert. *A Proper Drink: The Untold Story of How a Band of Bartenders Saved the Civilized Drinking World.* Berkeley: Ten Speed Press, 2016

Thomas, Jerry. *The Bar-Tenders Guide.* New York: Dick & Fitzgerald, 1862

Vermeire, Robert. *Cocktails: How to Mix Them.* London: Herbert Jenkins, 1922

Wondrich, David. *Imbibe! From Absinthe Cocktail to Whiskey Smash, a Salute in Stories and Drinks to "Professor" Jerry Thomas, Pioneer of the American Bar* (updated and revised ed.). New York: Perigee, 2015

Wondrich, David. *Punch: the Delights (and Dangers) of the Flowing Bowl.* New York: Perigee, 2010

Online

Alcademics (alcademics.com): Comprehensive, endearingly nerdy blog by drinks writer Camper English.

Cold Glass (cold-glass.com): Vivid thumbnail histories of a number of classic cocktails from amateur mixologist Doug Ford.

Difford's Guide (diffordsguide.com): Encyclopaedic collection of articles, cocktail recipes, and tasting notes.

Esquire drinks column by David Wondrich (esquire.com/author/3633/david-wondrich): Concise, potted histories of any number of classic cocktails, written by the world's preeminent drinks historian.

Exposition Universelle des Vins et Spiritueux (E.U.V.S.) Vintage Cocktail Books (euvs-vintage-cocktail-books.cld.bz): Scanned copies of any number of vintage cocktail books, many drawn from the private collection of drinks historians Anistatia Miller and Jared Brown.

Kindred Cocktails (kindredcocktails.com): Database of craft cocktail recipes, featuring lengthy and informative articles about a number of cocktails' histories.

Liquor.com articles by Gary Regan (liquor.com/author/gary-regan): Entertaining and informative short pieces from a true character of the drinks world.

PUNCH (punchdrink.com): In-depth features about drinking trends and an extensive collection of original cocktail recipes sourced from bars around the world.

About the Author

Chad Parkhill is a writer and bartender based in Melbourne, Australia. His work has appeared in *The Australian*, *The Lifted Brow*, *Kill Your Darlings*, *Meanjin*, and *The Quietus*, among others. He is currently the cocktail columnist for the *Guardian* Australia. *Around the World in 80 Cocktails* is his first book.

About the Illustrator

Alice Oehr is a designer from Melbourne, Australia whose distinct, colourful style incorporates her love of food, pattern, collage and drawing. Her designs have made their way into textiles, homewares, magazines, books, and even a series of six-foot-tall Ancient Egyptian statues for a marquee at Melbourne's Spring Racing Carnival. Travel and vintage posters are two of her favourite things.

Acknowledgements

First and foremost, my unending gratitude goes to Zora Sanders and Sue and Trevor Parkhill, without whose love and support this book could not have been written.

Thanks to the writers and bartenders whose work has informed and inspired the contents of this book: David Wondrich; Jared Brown and Anistatia Miller; Wayne Curtis; Jeff Berry; Gary Regan; Paul Clarke; Simon Difford; Doug Ford; Karen McNeil; Talia Baiocchi; Robert Simonson; Jeffrey Morgenthaler; Camper English; Dave Arnold; Toby Cecchini; Audrey Saunders; and too many others to do justice to properly in this space.

Thanks to the bars that provided their original recipes for this volume: Stephan Levan at Honi Honi; Andres Rolando at Harrison Speakeasy; Thanos Prunarus at Baba Au Rum; Bertil Tottenborg at Gustu; Stephanie Canfell at The Bowery; Irena Pogarcic at Hawksmoor; and Rolands Burtnieks at Bar XIII.

Thanks to the editors who have commissioned and otherwise encouraged my writing about booze: Chris Harms, Emily Williams and Zuzanna Napieralski at *Rave*; Ronnie Scott, Sam Cooney, and Stephanie Van Schilt at *The Lifted Brow*; Melanie Mahoney and Taryn Stenvei at Junkee; Steph Harmon at *The Guardian*; and David Wondrich at *The Oxford Companion to Spirits and Cocktails*.

Thanks to the editors at Hardie Grant Travel who shepherded this project through to completion: Lauren Whybrow and Melissa Kayser for commissioning it; Kate Armstrong for adeptly managing its progress and remaining a stalwart guide throughout; George Garner for streamlining my prose to its current sleek form; and Eugenie Baulch for proofreading it with such a keen eye. Thanks, too, to Grace West and Andy Warren for the beautiful internal design. A special thank you to Alice Oehr for the amazing illustrations – as well as for putting up with my pedantry about garnishes and glassware.

Finally, thanks to the team at Heartattack and Vine: Emily Bitto and Nathen Doyle, for the job that supported me while I wrote this book and for trusting me with their cocktail program; Matthew Roberts for the informative chats about cocktails and booze (and for putting me on to the Bird of Paradise); and the rest of the team for all the good times.

Published in 2017 by Hardie Grant Books, an imprint of
Hardie Grant Publishing

Hardie Grant Books (Melbourne)
Building 1, 658 Church Street
Richmond, Victoria 3121
hardiegrantbooks.com.au

Hardie Grant Books (London)
5th & 6th Floors
52–54 Southwark Street
London SE1 1UN
hardiegrantbooks.co.uk

A Cataloguing-in-Publication entry is available from the
catalogue of the National Library of Australia at www.nla.gov.au

Around the World in 80 Cocktails
ISBN 978 1 74117 518 9

Commissioning editors Melissa Kayser and Lauren Whybrow
Managing editor Marg Bowman
Project editor Kate J. Armstrong
Editor Georgina Garner
Design manager Mark Campbell
Designers Grace West and Andy Warren
Cartography Emily Maffei
Typesetter and prepress Megan Ellis
Proofreader Eugenie Baulch
Indexer Max McMaster
Production manager Todd Rechner
Production coordinator Rebecca Bryson

Colour reproduction by Splitting Image Colour Studio
Printed in China by 1010 Printing International Limited

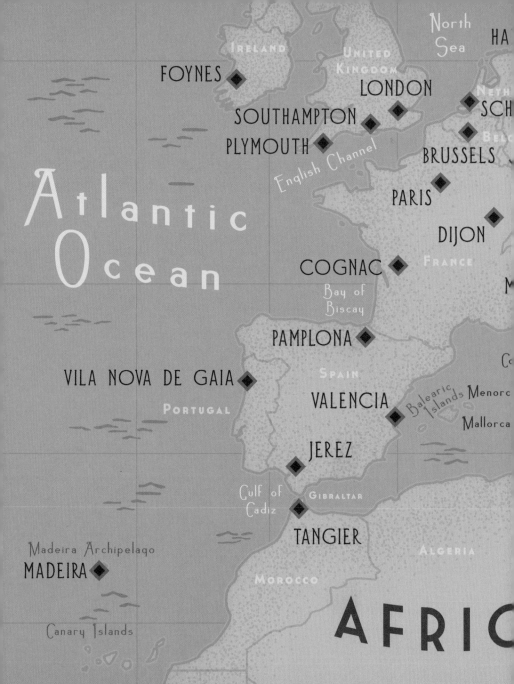